1500 EXTRAORDINARY FACTS

Ilia Moui

© 2023 Moui Ilia
All rights reserved.
Illustrations by Moui Ilia
Edition: Independently published
ISBN : 9798867129132

Acknowledgements

I would like to express my heartfelt gratitude to my wonderful wife and my two extraordinary children. Your support, your love, and your boundless curiosity have been my main source of inspiration throughout this intellectual journey.

What's the Plan?

Acknowledgements 2

What's the Plan? 3

Sneak Peek 6

Famous Explorers 13

Future Technologies 17

Underwater Discoveries 21

Mythology and Legends 26

Life in the Time of the Pharaohs 31

Unsolved Mysteries 35

Accidental Inventions 38

Fashion Through the Ages 42

Stars and Constellations 45

Famous Kings and Queens 48

Wonders of the World 51

Pirates and Their Hidden Treasures 54

Festivals and Traditions of the World 57

Superfoods and Nutrition 60

World Records 62

Legendary Athletes 67

Great Animal Migrations 70

Martial Arts of the World 73

Space Travel and Space Conquest 76

Magicians and Illusionists 78

The Age of Dinosaurs 81

World Music and Dances 83

Inventors and Their Creations 86

Great Writers and Their Works 89

Renewable Energies 92

The Great Civilizations 94

Haunted Places and Urban Legends 97

Traditional Games and Board Games 100

The Heroes of the Resistance 102

Weather Phenomena 106

Exotic Fruits and Vegetables 109

The Great Artists and Their Masterpieces 111

The Life of the Samurai 114

Historical Monuments 117

Wildlife 120

Balloon and Airship Journeys 123

The Great Scientists 124

World Cuisines 127

Lighthouses and Their Significance 130

The Fascinating World of Insects 133

History of the Olympic Games 136

The Evolution of Cartoons 139

The history of video games 142

The Superheroes Through the Ages 145

The Famous Boy Bands and Girl Groups 148

The Evolution of Popular Toys 151

Literary Sagas 154

Social Networks 157

Iconic Music Festivals 159

Iconic Movies and TV Shows 161

Cryptography and Secret Codes 164

The Human Body 166

The History of Cinema and Special Effects 169

Iconic Women in History 172

Sports 175

Music and Instruments 177

Science 180

Theater and Performance 183

Anthropology 186

Laws 189

Businesses 192

Politics 195

Flag 198

Medicine 201

Aliens and UFOs 204

The Power of Colors 207

Incredible Machines 210

The Castle 213

Unexplained Natural Phenomena 216

Lost Civilizations 218

Mathematics in Nature 221

Chess and Checkmate 224

The Art of Camouflage 227

The Months of the Year 230

Precious Stones 233

Street Art 236

Recycling 239

Modes of Transportation 242

Pets 244

Sneak Peek

The Great Wall of China is so vast that one might think it can be seen from the Moon, right? Wrong! Despite popular belief, it is not visible from the Moon with the naked eye.

The first-ever movie lasted only 2.11 minutes. Created by the Lumière brothers in 1895, it showed workers leaving their factory.

There's a sport called "underwater football." Yes, you heard that right! Players wear fins and use a weighted ball to score goals, all under water.

An octagon has eight sides, which makes sense. But do you know what a chiliagon is? It's a shape with 1,000 sides!

Giraffes have only two sleeping positions: standing or lying down in a ball. Even when they sleep standing up, they're ready to flee at a moment's notice.

Did you know that a single cell in your brain can hold five times more information than the Encyclopædia Britannica? That's enormous, considering this encyclopedia has about 40 million words on half a million topics! It's like having a massive library in your head!

Coffee was so vital in Ottoman culture that in 1475, there was a law allowing a woman to divorce if her husband did not provide her with enough coffee.

The oldest known piece of chewing gum is about 5,000 years old and was found in Sweden. Imagine chewing on something made before the pyramids!

In 1962, a submarine volcanic eruption near Iceland created a new island. It was named Surtsey, after a fire giant in Norse mythology.

The last meal served on the Titanic included ten courses, ranging from oysters to foie gras to roast duck.

The term "breakfast" in French actually means "breaking the fast." So, the next time you have breakfast, remember that you're ending a fast!

There's a poop museum in England. Yes, you read that correctly. The "Poo Museum" is dedicated to everything related to excrement.

Ants are incredibly strong for their size. They can carry up to 50 times their own weight. That's like a child carrying a car!

Rubies and sapphires are actually the same mineral, called corundum. The only difference between them is the color. Rubies are red due to traces of chromium in the corundum, while sapphires can be various colors (blue being the most well-known) due to traces of iron, titanium, or other elements.

A lightning bolt can heat the air around it to temperatures five times hotter than the surface of the sun. That's scorching!

Kangaroos cannot walk backward. Their body structure and long tail prevent them from doing so.

Snowflakes always have six branches. Not five, not seven, always six, due to the way water molecules crystallize.

The largest desert in the world is not the Sahara, but Antarctica! Although it's covered in ice, it's technically considered a desert due to its low precipitation.

There's an island so overrun with snakes it's called "Snake Island." It's located off the coast of Brazil, and it's illegal to visit without permission.

The longest word in the French language without a vowel is "crypts," a term meaning "underground cavities" or "hidden places."

There are more ways to shuffle a standard deck of cards than there are atoms on Earth. It's almost impossible to imagine!

If you lined up all the blood vessels in your body end to end, they could circle the Earth more than twice.

Bees are really smart, you know? They can even recognize human faces. Scientists conducted an experiment where they showed bees pictures of people. The bees learned which face would give them a sweet reward, like nectar. Isn't that incredible?

The eruption of the Krakatoa volcano in 1883 produced the loudest sound ever recorded. The noise was heard over 3,000 miles away, which is about 4,828 kilometers.

The full name of the city of Bangkok in Thailand is Krung Thep Mahanakhon Amon Rattanakosin Mahinthara Ayuthaya Mahadilok Phop Noppharat Ratchathani Burirom Udomratchaniwet Mahasathan Amon Piman Awatan Sathit Sakkathattiya Witsanukam Prasit. This incredibly long 169-character name holds the Guinness World Record for the longest place name.

Starfish don't have brains. They use a network of nerves to move and hunt, which is quite amazing for an animal without a brain.

Sunlight takes about 8 minutes and 20 seconds to reach Earth. So, when you look at the sun, you're seeing how it was a little over 8 minutes ago.

Play-Doh, beloved by children and artists, started as a cleaning product. That's right! Originally designed for cleaning wallpaper, it wasn't really effective. But when a teacher discovered it was perfect for art projects in class, a new use was found for it.

Velcro is another invention that owes its existence to a walk in nature. A Swiss engineer, Georges de Mestral, noticed how burdock seeds clung to his pants and his dog's fur. He was so fascinated that he decided to create a fastening mechanism that mimics this natural phenomenon.

Ever wondered why soap bubbles are round? Well, it's because of the water's surface tension! Water molecules attract each other, creating a spherical shape. It's the most efficient way for water to minimize its surface area.

The history of the Frisbee is just as fun! Did you know it was inspired by pie tins from a bakery? Students would throw these tins like discs, and the toy company Wham-O noticed this game and created the Frisbee we know today.

And let's not forget the Rubik's Cube, that puzzle that has fascinated generations. It was invented by Ernő Rubik, a Hungarian architect, to help his students understand spatial dimensions. He never imagined his toy would become a global phenomenon.

The crackling sound you hear when you break a chocolate bar is not by chance. The sound is the result of breaking the sugar and cocoa crystals in the chocolate. The clearer the sound, the better the quality of the chocolate!

Have you ever heard of Stendhal Syndrome? It's an intense physical and emotional reaction to an overdose of art or beauty, named after the French writer Stendhal. Imagine being so moved by a painting that your heart starts racing!

Next time you see a spider in the house, don't rush to squash it! Some spiders are actually great allies in the fight against pests. They can consume up to 2,000 insects a year!

Chewing gum has a fascinating history. Did you know it was originally made from tree sap? The Mayans used chicle, a form of natural rubber, as the base for their chewing gum.

The famous Nokia tune, which many of us associate with mobile phones, is actually a classical guitar composition called "Gran Vals," written by the Spanish musician Francisco Tárrega in 1902.

Pandas spend almost all their day eating bamboo, but did you know they have a carnivore's digestive system? It's a real biological mystery how these adorable creatures get enough nutrients from their bamboo meals!

The term "OK" comes from the phrase "Oll Korrect," a humorous way of misspelling "All Correct" in English.

It was popularized during Martin Van Buren's presidential campaign in 1840 and has become an integral part of our everyday language.

The deepest point in the oceans is the Mariana Trench, which is so deep that if Mount Everest were placed in it, its summit would still be over two kilometers underwater!

The Great Pyramid of Giza was once covered in white limestone, which reflected the sun. This made it shine like a "jewel" during the day, earning it the name "Khufu's Horizon."

Ketchup was originally a sauce made from fermented fish. Yes, you read that correctly! It was only much later that it was made with tomatoes.

Flamingos aren't actually pink. They are born gray, and their pink hue comes from their diet rich in beta-carotene, like shrimp and certain algae.

Have you ever heard of fish rain? It's a rare but real meteorological phenomenon where fish are sucked into clouds during a waterspout and then fall back down with the rain.

The oldest known board game to date is Senet, an Egyptian game that dates back to 3500 BCE. The exact rules have been lost to time, but replicas of the game are often found in Egyptian tombs.

Tattooing has an ancient and varied history. Tattoo marks have been found on Ötzi, the Iceman, who lived over 5,000 years ago!

Dolphins use sea sponges to protect their rostrums (their "noses") when foraging on the seabed. This is called tool use in animals, and it's quite rare.

The yeti, often called the abominable snowman, is a legendary creature of the Himalayas. Although many expeditions have been organized to find it, no conclusive evidence of its existence has been provided.

Did you know that koalas' fingerprints are so similar to humans' that they have been confused during criminal investigations?

The first elevator was installed in a New York department store in 1857. However, it wasn't an immediate success because people were afraid to use it.

The Eiffel Tower wasn't very popular among Parisians during its construction for the 1889 World's Fair. Many considered it a "metal monstrosity." Today, it's one of the most beloved and visited monuments in the world.

Unicorns, those mythical creatures, have diverse origins. In some cultures, they represent purity and grace, while in others, they are fierce creatures to be avoided.

The largest living organism on Earth is not a whale or a sequoia, but a network of underground fungi in Oregon, USA. It covers over 2,385 acres!

The smallest bone in the human body is the stapes, located in the inner ear. It's barely 0.1 inches (2.5 mm) long!

The yo-yo is one of the oldest toys in the world. It's believed to have been invented in ancient Greece over 2,500 years ago.

The "Chaos Theory" suggests that the flap of a butterfly's wings in Brazil can cause a tornado in Texas. Although this may seem exaggerated, the idea is that small changes can have large effects in complex systems.

Ants have a surprisingly long lifespan compared to their small size. Some queens can live up to 30 years, which is incredible for an insect!

The largest underground waterfall is located in Whiting's Cave in Tennessee, USA. It has a height of 145 feet (44 meters), which is quite impressive for a waterfall hidden beneath the Earth's surface.

The famous Barbie doll was invented by Ruth and Elliot Handler. They named the doll "Barbara Millicent Roberts" in honor of their daughter, Barbara. So, Barbie's full name is actually Barbara Millicent Roberts! It's like Barbie was part of their family.

Origami, the Japanese art of paper folding, was preceded by a similar practice in China, known as Zhezhi. Paper was invented in China, so it makes sense that the art of paper folding also originated there.

Chocolate was considered a currency in the ancient Maya and Aztec civilizations. Cocoa beans were so valuable that they were used to pay taxes!

The most spoken language in the world is not English, but Mandarin, with nearly a billion native speakers. English comes in third, after Spanish.

I hope these facts have surprised you and made you eager to learn more about our amazing world. Ready for the adventure?

Famous Explorers

Hold on tight, budding adventurers! Imagine landing on an unknown land with only a few hundred companions. That's exactly what Hernán Cortés did when he arrived in Mexico. But make no mistake, it wasn't just a walk in the park! Between last-minute alliances and misunderstandings that changed the course of history, Cortés managed to overthrow an entire empire! Incredible, right?

Even before Christopher Columbus set foot in America, the Vikings were already there! Led by Leif Erikson, these warriors from the North sailed to a place they called Vinland. It's like a "bonus level" in a video game, but in real life! Unfortunately, their stay didn't last long, but their adventure proves that there's always more to discover!

Who said explorers couldn't be women? Mary Kingsley proved otherwise by traveling through West Africa, and she wasn't there for tourism! She studied local cultures and even criticized colonialism of her time. A true model of courage and open-mindedness!

Imagine yourself at the helm of a ship, mapping places no one has ever seen! That was the daily life of James Cook. But beware, not everything was a smooth cruise: his last voyage took a tragic turn in Hawaii. A melancholic end for a man who gave so much to science and adventure.

Before the Spaniards arrived with their ships, the Canary Islands were home to the Guanches. After the conquest, their unique culture disappeared, like an old lost treasure. A true lesson on the importance of preserving local cultures.

Forget GPS and highways, the Silk Road was the "Google Maps" of the 2nd century BC until the 14th century! This complex network connected entire continents, allowing cultural and commercial exchanges. A real "Internet" before the Internet!

Lost in the Peruvian mountains, Machu Picchu was a mystery until Hiram Bingham put it back on the map. Imagine discovering a forgotten city! It's like finding the secret level in your favorite video game, but for real!

If you think your inflatable boat is cool, wait until you see the ships of Zheng He! This Chinese admiral traveled to more than 30 countries with boats that resembled small floating villages. An epic adventure across the seven seas!

Alexander wasn't just "great," he was huge! At least, his empire was. But even the greatest heroes have their limits. After reaching India, his exhausted troops convinced him to turn back. A reminder that even conquerors need rest!

Francisco de Orellana claimed to have met a tribe of legendary female warriors during his exploration of the Amazon River. True or false? The debate continues, but one thing is for sure: the Amazon is full of mysteries waiting to be discovered.

Can you really be a great explorer without knowing how to swim? Marco Polo proved you can! He spent nearly a quarter of a century traveling through Asia and even though his swimming skills were non-existent, his bravery knew no bounds. His encounter with Kublai Khan in China has become a legend, inspiring generations of adventurers after him.

Dive into the icy mystery of the Arctic with Sir John Franklin. He set out on an expedition to discover the Northwest Passage, an unexplored route. Unfortunately, he and his crew became one of the greatest mysteries in the history of exploration. Found decades later, frozen in the ice, their story reminds us of the risks explorers take to quench their thirst for knowledge.

Do you think climbing Everest is a small feat? Just ask Junko Tabei! In 1975, she became the first woman to reach the summit of the world's roof. Despite all obstacles, she never gave up. An inspiration for all women who dare to dream big.

Imagine being lost in Africa, exploring territories still unknown. That's what happened to David Livingstone. He disappeared for years searching for the source of the Nile and was found with the famous phrase: "Dr. Livingstone, I presume?". His love for Africa and his determination to explore make him a legend.

If you're fascinated by New Zealand, you can thank James Cook. This British captain was a pioneer in mapping this beautiful country. Along the way, he even managed to establish relationships with the Maoris. An adventure that has enriched our knowledge of the world.

Gold has always been a source of fascination, hasn't it? Hernán Cortés was just as fascinated, and it led him to the conquest of the Aztec Empire. His confrontations with Emperor Moctezuma II changed the course of history forever. But his legacy is complex, and the debate over his actions continues to this day.

If you think the race to reach the South Pole was just a walk in the snow, think again! Roald Amundsen outpaced his rival Robert Falcon Scott and was the first man to plant his flag there. His success was not just a personal victory, but a feat that highlighted the challenges and dangers of exploration in Antarctica.

Have you ever dreamed of becoming a diplomat or an explorer? Why not be both, like Gertrude Bell? Nicknamed the "Queen of the Desert," she played a key role in the creation of modern Iraq and forged relationships with many tribes in the Middle East. Her linguistic and diplomatic talents were so impressive that she remains an iconic figure to this day.

Imagine searching for a lost city in the Amazon jungle. That's exactly what Percy Fawcett attempted to do with his quest for the "City Z". Despite numerous expeditions, he never found the city and eventually disappeared in the jungle in 1925. His adventure adds a layer of mystery to an already fascinating story.

The history of exploration is full of firsts, and the first circumnavigation of the globe is a shining example. Even though Ferdinand Magellan didn't survive the voyage, his crew, led by Juan Sebastián Elcano, managed to complete this incredible adventure. A journey that definitively proved that the Earth is round.

Sometimes, you have to be bold to break barriers. Jeanne Baré, disguised as a man, boarded the expedition of Louis Antoine de Bougainville and became the first woman to circumnavigate the globe. An achievement that proved that courage knows no gender.

If you've ever been amazed by Canada, you owe a thank you to Jacques Cartier. This French explorer was the first European to map the Gulf of Saint Lawrence and claimed Canada for France. His adventure opened a new chapter in the history of New France.

David Livingstone was not just an explorer, he was also a mystery. He disappeared for years searching for the source of the Nile, before being found with the legendary words: "Dr. Livingstone, I presume?". A reminder that every adventure has its own legends.

Future Technologies

Imagine a world where your car knows exactly where you want to go and can even drive you there without you having to lift a finger. Autonomous electric cars aren't just a futuristic vision, they could well become the norm. Thanks to the magic of artificial intelligence, these cars will communicate with each other to avoid traffic jams and recharge without cables, using solar energy. Say goodbye to traffic jams and gas stations!

Have you ever found yourself running to the supermarket because your fridge was empty? In the future, your home could take care of all that for you. Smart homes will be like personal assistants, programmed to know your tastes and needs. Imagine windows that automatically darken depending on the weather or refrigerators that order food for you. The comfort of a button, or perhaps even a simple thought.

History classes could take on a whole new dimension. Rather than sitting in class listening to a teacher talk about ancient Egypt, why not take a virtual trip to see the pyramids yourself? Thanks to virtual reality, future students could explore distant worlds without ever leaving the classroom, making learning more interactive and memorable than ever.

The future of medicine could be revolutionized by bioprinting. Imagine hospitals equipped with 3D printers capable of creating human organs on demand, from living cells. No more long waiting lists for a transplant; each organ would be a custom creation.

The clothes of the future will be much more than just pieces of fabric. Imagine T-shirts capable of measuring your heart rate or shoes that generate electricity with each step. Fashion will no longer be just a matter of style, but also of functionality.

Nuclear fusion, once a distant dream, could become tomorrow's energy source. If this technology materializes, it would offer a clean and almost unlimited source of energy. Imagine entire cities powered without pollution or carbon emissions.

In a world where everything is instant, waiting several days for a delivery could soon become a thing of the past. Drones could take over, delivering your orders directly to your door in a few hours, or even minutes.

Farms could soon rise towards the sky rather than stretching as far as the eye can see. Vertical farms, built high in special structures, could revolutionize urban agriculture and reduce emissions related to food transport.

Who hasn't dreamed of roads that do more than just carry you from point A to point B? Roads made of solar panels could both facilitate transport and generate electricity. A two-in-one that would be a giant step towards more sustainable infrastructure.

Brain implants could one day allow you to learn a new skill in the blink of an eye. No need to spend years studying a new language or learning to play an instrument. A simple electronic chip, and you're done.

Your mirror could become your new fashion assistant. Thanks to connectivity and artificial intelligence, it could give you advice on your outfit of the day, depending on the weather or your schedule. No more morning wardrobe dilemmas.

Elevators could no longer be limited to simple vertical movement. Imagine elevators that also move horizontally, thanks to magnetic levitation. The skyscrapers of the future could resemble true three-dimensional labyrinths.

Hydroponics could become the new norm in agriculture. This technique, which allows plants to be grown without soil, offers higher yields and requires less space. Perfect for feeding an ever-growing global population.

Goodbye to frozen video calls on a screen! Holograms could allow face-to-face conversations, even when miles separate you. Remote meetings would then take on a whole new dimension.

In a world where time is money, trains could soon travel at supersonic speeds. Thanks to vacuum tubes, the Paris-New York journey could be done in less than an hour. Traveling to the other side of the world would no longer be an obstacle.

The buildings of the future could be designed to do much more than just shelter us. Imagine structures capable of absorbing carbon dioxide, thus contributing to the fight against climate change. Each building would become a silent soldier in the war against global warming.

Goodbye endless charging! The batteries of the future could recharge in seconds and last for weeks. Battery failures would thus become a nuisance of the past.

It wouldn't just be plants that capture solar energy. The windows of our homes could be designed to transform sunlight into electricity, making every building a mini-solar power plant.

Nanorobots could revolutionize medicine by directly targeting diseased cells. Microscopic robots could deliver drugs to cancer cells, sparing healthy cells and increasing the effectiveness of treatments.

"Neuroprostheses" could be used to restore or enhance human abilities, such as sight or hearing. Sophisticated devices could be implanted in the body, pushing the boundaries of what we consider "human."

CRISPR technology, which is a revolutionary tool scientists use to change genes, could be used to eliminate genetic diseases before birth. This would be a giant step in disease prevention and ensuring a healthier life for all.

Augmented reality could become an integral part of our daily lives. Digital information could be overlaid on our real environment via glasses or lenses, enriching our interaction with the world around us.

Smart contact lenses could replace our smartphones. Imagine, you could read your messages or check the weather without having to take out your phone. A simple blink of the eye, and the virtual world opens up to you.

Artificial intelligence could revolutionize the way we interact with animals. Special devices could translate barks or meows into human language. Thus, you would know exactly what your pet wants to tell you!

Virtual reality could also be used for environmental preservation. Imagine exploring the Amazon rainforest without leaving your room. You could even "plant" virtual trees that will then be planted in reality!

Speaking of trees, scientists are working on trees that glow in the dark. No need for streetlights, streets could be illuminated by bioluminescent trees!

Food packaging of the future could be completely edible. No more waste, you could eat your sandwich and its packaging. A real win for the planet!

Imagine artificial clouds that could be created to bring rain where it's most needed. Drought areas could then become fertile lands!

3D printers could be used to manufacture entire houses in a few hours. You could even choose the design of your room in a few clicks.

The future of video games is even more exciting. With special haptic gloves, you could feel the objects and textures of the game as if you were really touching them.

Drones could be used to replant forests. Equipped with seeds, they would fly over deforested areas and plant thousands of trees in a single day.

Underwater Discoveries

The deepest point known in the oceans, the Mariana Trench, plunges over 10,000 meters below the surface. James Cameron, famous for directing the movie "Titanic," ventured alone into these depths in 2012.

At the bottom of the seas are brine pools, expanses of extremely salty water. These underwater lakes have a unique composition and are home to equally unique forms of life.

The legendary wreck of the Titanic, which sank in 1912, was found in 1985 by Dr. Robert Ballard. Resting at nearly 3,800 meters deep, this ship is a poignant testament to maritime history.

Stretching over 2,300 kilometers, Australia's Great Barrier Reef is the planet's largest coral reef system. Its expanse is such that it is visible from space.

The year 2019 was marked by the discovery of a giant squid (about 3 to 4 meters) in the depths of the Gulf of Mexico, specifically at 750 meters below the surface. This find adds another layer of mystery to the biodiversity of the abyss.

Compared to terrestrial mountains, underwater mountains are just as impressive. For example, if Mauna Kea in Hawaii were measured from its oceanic base, it would surpass Everest in height.

Submerged cities are not just legends. The lost city of Thonis-Heracleion was discovered off the coast of Egypt, submerged for over a millennium. This place offers a window into ancient civilizations and their relationship with the sea.

The Pacific "Ring of Fire" is an arc of geoactivity known for its earthquakes and volcanic eruptions. It is also home to hydrothermal vents that eject hot fluids saturated with minerals.

In 2020, a new species of jellyfish was identified in the Mariana Trench, proving that the mysteries of the deep sea are far from being all resolved.

The Black Sea has an astonishing feature: an anoxic water layer beyond 150 meters deep. This lack of oxygen has the effect of remarkably well preserving wrecks, thus offering a treasure for maritime archaeologists.

The internet we use daily relies largely on a vast network of underwater cables. They stretch for hundreds of thousands of kilometers and ensure communications between continents.

Tamu Massif, the largest known underwater volcano, hides in the Pacific Ocean. Its area is almost comparable to that of the state of New Mexico.

Methane hydrates, reserves of frozen methane, are scattered on the seabed. They could represent a future source of energy, but their exploitation raises environmental questions.

The hydrothermal springs of the depths are home to creatures capable of living in extreme conditions, such as high temperatures and high levels of toxicity.

In 2018, an astonishing seaweed forest was discovered near Antarctica. Hidden for millennia, it reminds us how much the seabed remains unexplored territory.

Surprising aquatic phenomena, such as "lakes" and "rivers" underwater, exist due to variations in salinity. These areas even have their own "waves," a curiosity that amazes researchers.

The wreck of the USS Indianapolis, sunk in 1945, was located in 2017 at a dizzying depth of over 5,500 meters. This American warship rests in the Pacific Ocean.

The Baltic Sea is a treasure trove of marine archaeology, harboring a large number of well-preserved wrecks. This preservation is partly due to its low salinity, which slows decomposition.

In 2015, a major archaeological discovery was made off the Greek coast: a submerged city dating back 5,000 years. This find sheds new light on ancient civilizations and the rise of the waters.

Some sharks, like the Greenland shark, have evolved to live in extreme depths, often exceeding 2,200 meters. These adapted creatures teach us more about the limits of life in hostile environments.

Alvin, a research submarine, has made over 4,400 dives, allowing scientists to study the seabed like never before. Discoveries in geology, biology, and underwater archaeology have been made possible thanks to this tool.

Icebergs are not just drifting masses of ice. Below the water's surface, they can have eroded bases, forming caverns and tunnels that are true works of natural art.

In the abyssal darkness, some fish, such as lanternfish or anglerfish, have developed the ability to produce their own light. This phenomenon, called bioluminescence, allows them to attract their prey in total darkness.

The Dead Sea, known for its exceptional salinity, is home to unique microbial structures called "mats." These formations create strange underwater landscapes and are a subject of study for microbiologists.

Underwater caves, such as the famous Blue Hole in Belize, offer a unique look at marine geology and ecosystems. They are often the scene of important scientific discoveries.

In 2019, a Dumbo octopus was observed at a record depth in the Mariana Trench. This observation challenges our knowledge of the limits of life in the abyss.

Underwater internet cables are not buried. In fact, most simply rest on the ocean floor. Special ships lay them out over thousands of kilometers.

Octopuses have three hearts and their blood is blue! They are incredibly intelligent creatures that can solve puzzles and even escape from their aquariums.

Corals are not just plants. In fact, they are a symbiosis between an algae and an animal. Coral reefs are like the "rainforests of the sea," housing up to 25% of all known marine species.

Bull sharks are capable of surviving in both fresh and saltwater. They have been found swimming up rivers like the Amazon.

The "Point Nemo" is the point in the ocean furthest from any land. It is so isolated that astronauts on the International Space Station pass closer to this point than anyone on Earth!

The Megalodon, a prehistoric shark, had teeth that could measure up to 18 centimeters. Imagine a shark so large it could swallow a bus!

The kraken, a legendary creature resembling a giant octopus, is a myth born from sailors' stories. Today, it is thought to be inspired by actual sightings of giant squids.

Dolphins use elaborate fishing techniques and often work as a team to gather and catch fish. They are also known for their intelligence and ability to communicate with each other.

Mythology and Legends

In Greek mythology, Icarus symbolizes hubris and the dangers of excessive ambition. Ignoring his father Daedalus' advice, he flew too close to the sun, causing his wax wings to melt and his fall into the Aegean Sea.

The Minotaur, born from the union between a queen and a sacred bull, was locked in a labyrinth designed by Daedalus. Theseus, aided by Ariadne and her ball of thread, managed to kill the creature and escape, turning the labyrinth into a tomb for the Minotaur.

Fenrir, the monstrous wolf of Norse mythology, is a terrifying figure. Chained by the gods who fear his power, he is destined to break his bonds at Ragnarök, the end of the world, to devour the sun and the moon.

The legend of Kuchisake-onna, the slit-mouthed woman, is a frightening Japanese urban legend. She asks passersby a deceptive question and then reveals her mutilated face, putting her victims in a deadly dilemma.

King Midas, famous for his touch that turns everything to gold, is a tragic example of human greed. The gift turns out to be a curse when Midas turns his own daughter into a gold statue.

The quest for the Holy Grail, the chalice that collected Christ's blood, is a central element of Arthurian legend. Only Galahad, the pure knight, manages to find the Grail, illustrating the notion of spiritual quest and purity.

In China, the dragon is revered as a symbol of power, wisdom, and good fortune. Unlike Western dragons, often seen as malevolent, the Chinese dragon is a benefactor and protector.

The Chupacabra, a creature from Latin American folklore, is often blamed for attacks on livestock. Its name means "goat sucker" in Spanish, and it is often described as a reptilian monster with spines or scales.

Osiris, in Egyptian mythology, is the god of death and resurrection. Murdered by his brother Seth, he is brought back to life by his wife Isis and becomes the judge of souls in the afterlife.

The Morrigan, the Celtic goddess of war and fate, is a complex figure associated with death and regeneration. She can take the form of a crow or an old woman, and she often plays a role in prophecies of war and death.

Medusa, one of the Gorgons, is famous for her snake hair and petrifying gaze. Perseus manages to defeat her by using a shield as a mirror, thus avoiding her deadly gaze.

In Hinduism, avatars of Vishnu, such as Rama and Krishna, embody moral and spiritual principles. They appear in times of great cosmic imbalance to restore order and justice.

Baba Yaga, the Slavic witch, is an ambiguous figure. Sometimes malevolent, sometimes wise, she lives in a hut mounted on chicken legs and flies in a mortar. She is often consulted for advice, but at your own risk.

Maui, the Polynesian hero, is known for his incredible feats, like fishing up the North Island of New Zealand. Using his magical hook, he pulled this land from the ocean floor, creating a home for his people.

The Phoenix, a mythical bird, is a symbol of rebirth. At the end of its life, it bursts into flames and is reborn from its ashes, thus embodying the eternal cycles of death and rebirth.

Cerberus, the three-headed dog, guards the gates of Hades in Greek mythology. He prevents the dead from escaping and the living from entering, acting as a guardian between the two worlds.

In Japanese folklore, the Tanuki is a cunning animal, capable of transforming and playing tricks. It is often depicted with a straw hat and a bottle of sake, symbols of its jovial nature.

Janus, the Roman god of doors and passages, has two faces to look both at the past and the future. He is often invoked at the beginning of new ventures to bring success and happiness.

The Valkyries, divine warriors of Norse mythology, choose the bravest warriors fallen in battle to take them to Valhalla, which is located within the realm of the gods where they prepare for Ragnarök.

The unicorn, often associated with purity and magic, is a mythical creature that continues to captivate the imagination. In legend, only a pure-hearted being can approach a unicorn.

The Dreamtime, in Aboriginal mythology, is a time when ancestral beings formed the Earth. It is considered a sacred time and is central to the world understanding of Aboriginal peoples.

Anubis, the Egyptian god with a dog's head, plays a crucial role in funeral rituals. He weighs the hearts of the deceased against a feather of Maat to determine their fate in the afterlife.

The chimera is a composite creature from Greek mythology, usually represented with a lion's body, a goat's head, and a snake's tail. It is a figure of destruction, spewing fire and ravaging lands.

Mermaids, half-woman, half-fish creatures, are famous for their enchanting song that lures sailors to their doom. Their legend has been immortalized in stories like the Odyssey, where Odysseus resists their call by being tied to the mast of his ship.

Quetzalcoatl, the feathered serpent of Aztec mythology, is a god of creation, wind, and knowledge. He is often opposed to Tezcatlipoca, his brother and adversary, in mythological stories.

According to Irish mythology, leprechauns are small mischievous beings who hide their gold at the end of rainbows. Catching a leprechaun is a difficult task, but if successful, he can grant three wishes to his captor.

Hephaestus, the Greek god of the forge, is known for his great artisanal skill. Although physically handicapped, he creates beautiful objects, like the armor of gods and heroes.

Pele, the Hawaiian goddess of fire and volcanoes, is a powerful and unpredictable figure. She is both a creator and a destroyer, shaping the islands through volcanic eruptions while threatening to destroy them.

The Kappa, aquatic creatures from Japanese mythology, are both feared and respected. They challenge humans in wrestling duels and are known for their love of cucumbers.

In Scandinavian mythology, trolls are often misunderstood creatures. Although they are considered evil giants in some stories, they are also sometimes seen as solitary and melancholy beings.

The Manticore, originating from Persian mythology, is a terrifying creature with the body of a lion, a human head, and a scorpion's tail. It is often associated with death and destruction.

Echidna, the "mother of all monsters" in Greek mythology, gave birth to many formidable creatures, like the Sphinx and Cerberus. She is often described as a creature half-woman, half-serpent.

Anansi, the cunning spider from African mythology, is a trickster hero who uses his intelligence to overcome seemingly insurmountable obstacles. His stories are lessons in cunning and ingenuity.

The basilisk, a legendary serpent or dragon, has the power to kill with its gaze. It is so venomous that its breath and gaze can be deadly, and it can only be killed by its own reflection or the crowing of a rooster.

The Moai of Easter Island are gigantic stone statues that continue to fascinate researchers and tourists. According to legend, they were created to honor the ancestors and gods of the island.

Sedna, the Inuit goddess of the sea, is a tragic figure betrayed by her family. Thrown into the sea by her father, she becomes the mistress of marine creatures and a goddess revered by the Inuits.

The Griffin, a creature with the body of a lion and the head of an eagle, is a symbol of protection and majesty. It appears in various cultures and is often used as a royal emblem.

The Gargoyle, originating from French mythology, is a hybrid creature that spews water to ward off evil spirits. Gargoyles are often carved on cathedrals to serve as gutters and to ward off evil.

Life in the Time of the Pharaohs

Surprisingly, it was not slaves who built the imposing pyramids, but skilled and well-paid workers. They even had access to medical care. The artisans' pride was such that they left graffiti inside the pyramids, like invisible signatures, testifying to their lives and achievements.

Speaking of achievements, the meticulous process of mummification took up to 70 days. A special hook was inserted through the nose to remove the brain, a detail that might make even the bravest among us a little uneasy.

And did you know that Cleopatra, the famous pharaoh, was not of Egyptian origin? This powerful woman came from Greece, but she ruled Egypt with a passion and zeal that make her unforgettable.

The next time you chop an onion, think about its meaning to the ancient Egyptians: they saw in its concentric rings eternity itself.

In another register, the simple act of killing a cat, even accidentally, could lead you to the death penalty. Cats were sacred, and some were even mummified to accompany them in the afterlife.

The pharaohs, these almost divine rulers, had a sweet tooth. Honey was found in their tombs, a sweet gift for the gods and a way to preserve their bodies for eternity.

They were also fond of beauty and care, using Kohl, a mineral powder, to accentuate their eyes, a gesture they believed protective against diseases.

The Nile, this water vein that runs through Egypt, was more than just a source of irrigation. It also served as a crucial trade route. And speaking of ways, it is the Rosetta Stone that paved the way for the understanding of Egyptian hieroglyphs, this mysterious writing system that has long eluded decipherment.

You would be surprised to know that beer was part of the daily diet of Egyptians. Very different from modern beer, it was thick, a bit lumpy, and often sipped with a straw.

In the afterlife, clay figurines called "ushabtis" accompanied the pharaohs. They believed that these little statues would help them in their tasks in the afterlife.

The heart was for them the seat of the soul and emotions. It was so important that it remained in the body even after mummification.

Hieroglyphs, these complex writings, could be traced in all directions: horizontally, vertically, from right to left or from left to right.

If you were impressed by the colossus of Ramses II in Memphis, know that it is more than 10 meters high, a stone feat that defies imagination. The "Djed pillars", these symbols of stability, are supposed to represent the spine of Osiris, the god of the afterlife.

Papyrus, this humble but robust plant, was used to create paper. Careful hammering and weaving transformed its fibers into a writing surface. Schools were often linked to temples, where priests were the educators.

In ancient Egypt, there was a very popular game called "senet". It was a bit like a mix of our chess and ludo games today. Pharaohs and very important people liked to play it. To win at senet, you had to be clever and think about your moves, like in chess, but you also had to have a bit of luck, like when you roll the dice in ludo. It was a very popular game a very, very long time ago!

The world of ancient Egypt is an open book of curiosities and wonders, a testament to the complexity and grandeur of human civilization. From advanced medicine to metaphysics, from papyrus shoes to animal-shaped oil lamps, each fragment of their life draws us into a vortex of fascination.

Beetle-shaped amulets were very popular and symbolized rebirth and protection. These small objects were often worn around the neck or embedded in jewelry, a constant sign of divine presence in everyday life.

Speaking of everyday life, Egyptians used oil lamps to light their homes once the sun went down. These lamps were often shaped like animals or deities, each detail being a tribute to their natural or spiritual environment.

The marital life of the pharaohs was just as fascinating. Although they had several wives, there was always a main queen. This woman had a special role to play, not only in the royal court but also in religious rituals. She was often seen as the earthly representative of the goddess Isis.

The lotus, this sublime flower, was a powerful symbol of purity and creation. Its image is omnipresent in Egyptian art, from wall frescoes to jewelry. Its dazzling whiteness evokes a sense of divinity and eternity.

Bread in Egypt was not the soft type we know today. It was often made with whole grains and even small pebbles, which tended to prematurely wear down the Egyptians' teeth. A small consolation, perhaps, for the dentists of the time who already had a good level of skill.

Medicine in Egypt was surprisingly advanced. Texts have survived, detailing surgical procedures, pharmacological remedies, and even dental practices. This is a field where the ancient Egyptians were undoubtedly pioneers.

Thebes, the "city of a hundred gates", was one of the most important cities. It was often the center of political and religious intrigue, and its architectural wealth makes it a fascinating subject of study for today's Egyptologists.

The mirror was a luxury item, often made of polished bronze. It was not only a tool of vanity, but also a symbol of sunlight, reflecting beauty and divinity.

Incense played a crucial role in Egyptian rituals. It was burned as an offering to the gods and used to purify temples. Its rising smoke was considered the very breath of the deities, a gateway between heaven and earth.

The Sphinx of Giza, this enigmatic statue, is often associated with the pharaoh Khafre, although controversies remain. This monument, half-man, half-lion, guards its secrets with disconcerting resistance.

Shaving one's head was a common practice to avoid lice infestations. Wigs, often luxurious and well-made, were worn as a sign of social status.

The color blue, so often present in Egyptian art and jewelry, was sacred. It evoked the sky, the realm of the gods, and symbolized wisdom and divinity. It was more than just a color; it was the emblem of a world beyond ours.

So, what do you think of these new revelations? Are they surprising, enlightening, or perhaps even both? Each fact, each detail, draws us deeper into the complexity of Egyptian civilization, a journey through time that amazes and inspires.

Unsolved Mysteries

The Bermuda Triangle, this maritime space flanked between Miami, Puerto Rico, and Bermuda, is an area of disquieting reputation. The planes and ships that disappear there without a trace have become the protagonists of an invisible drama. While some evoke magnetic anomalies, others lean towards particular meteorological phenomena. In any case, the mystery remains intact.

Let's move from the mysterious waters of the Atlantic to the depths of Loch Ness in Scotland, where the monster nicknamed "Nessie" continues to elude scientific investigations. The existence of this creature is a mystery that fuels legends and fascinates researchers. The dark waters of the lake seem to jealously guard their secret.

In wheat fields, strange patterns sometimes appear overnight. These crop circles are ephemeral works of art whose origin remains a puzzle. While some see the hand of talented pranksters, others suggest more esoteric explanations.

The disappearance of Malaysia Airlines MH370 in 2014 is a modern puzzle that has not yet been solved. Despite intensive searches and millions of dollars spent, the plane and its passengers remain untraceable. It's a mystery that has captivated the entire world, and to this day, defies any rational explanation.

Area 51, this isolated military base in the Nevada desert, is the subject of many conspiracy theories. From extraterrestrial activities to secret experiments, the speculations are as numerous as the security barriers surrounding the base. The American government may deny it, but the mystery only thickens.

Have you ever heard of the giant statues of Easter Island, these Moai that pose more questions than they offer answers? How could an isolated civilization have created these colossal monoliths without the aid of modern technologies? The mystery is far from being resolved, and the statues remain the silent guardians of ancient secrets.

The lost city of Atlantis, this immortal myth, was first described by the philosopher Plato. Since then, the location of this legendary city has given rise to numerous speculations. Is it a purely mythological creation, or a submerged city still waiting to be discovered? The debates are far from over.

The Lady of Elche, this enigmatic statue discovered in Spain, is an archaeological mystery. Its origin and meaning are subjects of academic debate. Is she a deity, a great queen, or a symbol of a forgotten culture? Researchers are divided, and the Lady remains silent.

The Mary Celeste, this ship found drifting in 1872 without a single crew member on board, is another maritime mystery. The vessel was in perfect condition, and the cargo intact. Where had the crew gone? Theories abound, but the truth remains elusive.

The Nazca Lines in Peru are another enigma that has not yet revealed all its secrets. These massive geoglyphs, visible only from the skies, have intrigued researchers for generations. What was the purpose of these monumental drawings, and how were they created with such precision? The answers to these questions remain as elusive as the figures themselves.

Moving from the Peruvian soil to the cryptic universe of the Voynich manuscript. This mysterious book, written in an indecipherable language, is a puzzle for cryptographers and linguists. Despite numerous attempts to decode it, the manuscript jealously guards its mystery. This grimoire, which seems straight out of a fantasy tale, is an enigma in itself.

The history of aviation also has its share of mysteries, like the disappearance of the legendary aviator Amelia Earhart. In 1937, she embarked on a journey around the world and disappeared without a trace. Despite countless theories, her fate remains an unresolved mystery. Amelia's heroism and the enigma of her disappearance continue to fascinate.

Stonehenge in England is another archaeological mystery that arouses curiosity and wonder. This prehistoric monument, made up of massive megaliths, is a real puzzle for researchers. How were these gigantic stones transported and assembled? And what was the purpose of this place? The mystery endures, shrouded in the fog of the English moor.

In Vietnam, the Tower of Hanoi is surrounded by legends and myths. Some consider it a magical object, while others see it as a site linked to ancient rituals. This mysterious edifice, which seems to be a gateway to the unknown, attracts the attention of the curious and researchers.

The case of the Tamam Shud man in Australia is just as troubling. This mystery, concerning an unidentified individual found dead on a beach, remains unsolved. A piece of paper found on him bore the words "Tamam Shud", adding an additional layer to this enigma. Who was this man, and what is the story behind these mysterious words?

The village of Roanoke in the United States is another mystery that blurs the boundary between history and legend. In 1590, all its inhabitants disappeared without a trace, except for the word "CROATOAN" carved on a tree. This word is the only clue in this troubling puzzle, and the history of the village remains an unsolved enigma.

The search for the treasure of Oak Island in Canada is a quest that has lasted for centuries. Many have searched it in quest of riches, but the treasure remains elusive. Is it a legend, or is there really a treasure hidden somewhere in the depths of this island?

Accidental Inventions

Silver nitrate, used in modern photography, owes its discovery to the alchemist Albertus Magnus. In attempting to transmute metals into gold, he stumbled upon this light-reactive substance.

The batik technique in Indonesia, where wax is used to create patterns on fabric, originated when an artisan accidentally spilled wax on a cloth. When dyeing it, he noticed that the wax prevented the dye from penetrating, thus creating a unique pattern.

Penicillin, often cited as an accidental discovery, paved the way for a whole class of antibiotics. Its discoverer, Alexander Fleming, could never have imagined that his Penicillium fungus would have such an impact on modern medicine.

The Frisbee was created from a simple plastic plate. Bored students began throwing the plate, realizing that it flew in a stable manner. The rest, as they say, is history.

Tailor's chalk, an indispensable tool for tailors, was invented when it was noticed that the remnants of construction chalk marked fabric very well and could be easily removed.

The smoke detector, so common today, was accidentally invented by an engineer working on a completely different project. Noticing how the smoke from his cigarette interfered with his experiments, he realized the potential of this discovery.

Fireworks, although initially used for military purposes in China, were discovered when chemists accidentally mixed saltpeter, sulfur, and charcoal, creating an explosive powder.

The technique of glass blowing, which revolutionized glass making, was discovered when an artisan accidentally dropped a hot metal tube into a pot of molten glass. In trying to retrieve it by blowing into the tube, he created a glass bubble.

The discovery of static electricity dates back to antiquity, when Greeks rubbed amber against wool and noticed that it attracted light objects. This simple act laid the foundation for our understanding of electricity.

Velox, a photographic paper developed by Leo Baekeland, was created while searching for a way to make paper insensitive to light. Instead, he discovered a paper that was extremely sensitive to light, which was perfect for the rapid development of photographs.

The invention of the cardiac pacemaker is another striking example of an accidental invention. Originally, engineer Wilson Greatbatch was working on a device to record heartbeats. After mistakenly inserting a resistor of the wrong size into his device, he realized that the device emitted a rhythm that perfectly mimicked the beat of a human heart.

Gore-Tex, the waterproof and breathable material we all know, was discovered when Wilbert L. Gore and his son Robert were experimenting with stretched polytetrafluoroethylene. The result was a material that could repel water while allowing air to pass, a boon for outdoor clothing.

The car horn, now a standard element of road safety, was invented by accident. An engineer working on early automobiles discovered that the shrill noise produced by the exhaust pipe could be used to warn pedestrians and other vehicles.

The hamster wheel, this iconic toy for our rodent friends, is the result of a fortuitous observation. An inventor noticed that his hamster liked to run in a small tunnel. By adding a curvature to this tunnel, he created the first hamster wheel.

The melody of the famous Beatles song "Yesterday" came to Paul McCartney in a dream. He woke up with the melody in his head and quickly recorded a demo so as not to forget it. This piece has become one of the most covered songs in history.

The origin of the microwave comes from an accident involving chocolate. Engineer Percy Spencer was working on radars during World War II when he noticed that the chocolate bar in his pocket had melted. Intrigued, he experimented further and came up with the invention of the microwave oven.

The principle of serotherapy was discovered when Albert Calmette and Camille Guérin accidentally inoculated a laboratory assistant with snake venom. To counter the effects, they injected him with serum from an immunized animal, thus saving his life.

Roy Plunkett was working on refrigerant gases when he discovered a white, slippery substance that resisted heat and chemicals. That's how Teflon was discovered.

James Schlatter was looking to create a medication for stomach ulcers when he accidentally discovered a sweet taste on his fingers. It was aspartame, a sweetener.

Wilhelm Röntgen was experimenting with cathode tubes when he accidentally discovered a kind of ray capable of passing through solid objects. That's how X-rays were discovered.

George Crum, a chef, created chips by accident. A customer complained that his potatoes were too thick and not crispy enough. In trying to please him, Crum cut the potatoes very thinly, fried them, and salted them. The customer loved them, and that's how chips were born.

Charles Goodyear was trying to make rubber more durable when he accidentally mixed sulfur with natural rubber and heated it. That's how the vulcanization of rubber was discovered.

John Stith Pemberton, an American pharmacist, was suffering from pain following war injuries and was looking to create a remedy to alleviate his discomfort. His experiment with coca and kola nut extracts led him to develop a tonic drink. This drink, originally intended to relieve his pain, became the famous soft drink Coca-Cola.

At 3M, Spencer Silver was looking to create a super glue, but he ended up creating a glue that stuck but could also be easily removed. His colleague Art Fry used this glue to create Post-it Notes.

Fashion Through the Ages

Sportswear, once reserved for physical activity, has made its way into everyday fashion over the past few decades. "Athleisure," a blend of athletic and leisure wear, has become a style in its own right, popularized by celebrities like Rihanna and Kanye West.

Nineteenth-century ball gowns were often equipped with crinolines, those large steel cages worn under the skirt to give it volume. They were the height of elegance, but also very cumbersome and uncomfortable.

In the 2000s, flip-flops transitioned from simple beach footwear to a fashion accessory, even worn in the city. While initially intended to protect feet from hot sand, they have become a style choice.

The bowler hat, made famous by characters like Charlie Chaplin, was originally a rigid hat designed to protect riders' heads. Over time, it has become a symbol of British elegance.

The 1980s saw the rise of the "preppy" look, inspired by the outfits of Ivy League university students. Polos, cardigans, and loafers were the mainstays of this style.

In the Middle Ages, both men and women wore "hose," stockings that were attached to a belt. It was not until the 16th century that the concept of "trousers" emerged, rendering hose obsolete.

Tattoos, which have a long history as forms of cultural expression, were adopted by Western fashion in the 20th century. Initially associated with sailors and bikers, they are now a popular style choice for all sorts of people.

In the 18th century, children's clothing was often miniature replicas of adult clothing. It wasn't until the 19th century that the concept of "children's clothing" really took off, with more practical and comfortable outfits.

In the 1990s, "unisex" clothing gained popularity. Inspired by the grunge movement, this style emphasized comfort and functionality rather than gender distinction.

The "little black dress," popularized by Coco Chanel in the 1920s, has become a staple of the female wardrobe. Its simplicity and elegance make it a versatile choice for many occasions.

Culottes, a cross between a skirt and trousers, were a real revolution in women's wardrobes. Originally designed to give women more freedom of movement, they have become a bold and versatile style option.

The fashion for "luxury sneakers" has taken the haute couture world by storm. Once confined to sports fields, sneakers have transformed into objects of desire branded by prestigious labels like Gucci or Louis Vuitton.

Maternity wear has undergone a radical transformation over the decades. In the past, pregnant women were expected to wear loose and unflattering clothes. Today, maternity fashion is designed to highlight the silhouette while offering comfort and functionality.

Punk fashion, born in the 1970s, was more than just a fashion trend. With its safety pins, mohawks, and studded leathers, it embodied a true attitude of rebellion against the system.

Overalls, originally designed as utilitarian workwear, have found their place in mainstream fashion. They became popular in the 1990s and have made a strong comeback recently, even worn by celebrities.

The rise of the zero-waste movement has also influenced fashion. Clothing made from recycled materials or brands advocating sustainability are increasingly popular, reflecting an ecological awareness.

The Pashmina scarf, originally from Kashmir, has transcended its cultural roots to become a global fashion accessory. It is appreciated for its softness and versatility, able to be worn in different ways.

In the 19th century, wearing a hat was almost mandatory in public. Whether it was the top hat for men or the bonnet for women, the hat was considered a sign of respectability.

The 2000s saw the emergence of "fast fashion," an approach to fashion that relies on rapid and low-cost production to keep up with the latest trends. Although controversial for its ethical and environmental implications, this approach has transformed the fashion industry.

Buttons, which we consider a standard element on clothing, were once a luxury. In the Middle Ages, only the wealthy could afford clothing with buttons, which were often made of precious materials like ivory or mother-of-pearl.

Stars and Constellations

Constellations are true celestial frescoes, starry narratives that mark the passage of time and seasons. They are the silent witnesses of myths and legends that have shaped our understanding of the world.

Ursa Minor, or the Little Bear, is often overlooked in favor of its big sister, the Great Bear. Yet, it houses the North Star, which has guided sailors and explorers for centuries. In mythology, it represents Arcas, the son of the nymph Callisto, transformed into a bear by Zeus.

Draco, the Dragon, winds through the night sky near the Little and Great Bears. According to legend, it is the dragon killed by Cadmus, the founder of Thebes. Another story links it to Ladon, the dragon that guarded the golden apples in the Garden of the Hesperides.

Virgo, or the Virgin, is one of the largest constellations in the zodiac. It is often associated with Demeter, the Greek goddess of agriculture, or Astraea, the goddess of Justice. Its brightest star, Spica, has been used in navigation and agriculture to mark the beginning of planting seasons.

Taurus, the Bull, is a dominant constellation in the winter sky. It represents the bull in which Zeus abducted Europa. The star Aldebaran, the eye of the bull, is one of the brightest stars of the night.

Aries, the Ram, is linked to the story of the Golden Fleece, which saved Phrixus and Helle. In the zodiac, it marks the beginning of spring and an annual renewal.

Sagittarius, the Archer, is often depicted as a centaur holding a bow and arrow. It is sometimes associated with Chiron, although the latter is usually identified with the constellation Centaurus.

Ophiuchus, the Serpent Bearer, is a constellation often forgotten because it is not part of the traditional zodiac. However, it is related to Asclepius, the Greek god of medicine, who learned the secrets of life and death by observing a serpent.

Hercules, although less bright than other star groups, is nonetheless significant. He is the hero of several myths and legends, and his name is immortalized in the sky for his many feats.

Aquila, the Eagle, is associated with the bird that Zeus sent to retrieve Prometheus's liver. Its main star, Altair, forms with Vega and Deneb, a summer asterism known as the Summer Triangle.

Orion, the Hunter, is one of the most recognizable constellations, with its belt of three bright stars. Associated with the Greek hero Orion, it is also present in other mythologies, such as that of ancient Egypt where it was linked to Osiris, the god of the afterlife.

Cassiopeia, the Queen, is easily identifiable by its "W" or "M" shape, depending on its orientation in the sky. In Greek mythology, Cassiopeia was the vain queen of Ethiopia who unleashed the wrath of Poseidon. Today, it serves as a landmark for astronomers and starry sky enthusiasts.

Andromeda, the Princess, is associated with the daughter of Cassiopeia and Cepheus, saved from the sea monster Cetus by Perseus. The Andromeda Galaxy, our neighbor, takes its name from this constellation and reminds us of the immensity of the universe.

Cygnus, the Swan, is also known as the Northern Cross. It is associated with several legends, including Zeus transforming into a swan or Phaeton, the son of the Sun god, who was turned into a swan to escape the wrath of Zeus.

Scorpius, the Scorpion, is the protagonist of one of the most famous stories of Greek mythology. Sent by Gaia or Artemis according to the versions, it stings and kills Orion to put an end to his destructive fury on the animals. After their death, the two adversaries are placed on opposite sides of the sky to avoid further conflicts.

Lynx is a lesser-known constellation, created by Johannes Hevelius in the 17th century. The name comes from the fact that, according to Hevelius, one would need the eyes of a lynx to see its faintly luminous stars.

The hunting dogs, Canes Venatici, were once considered part of the Great Bear. Also created by Johannes Hevelius, it is often associated with the hunting dogs of Artemis or Diana in Roman mythology.

Famous Kings and Queens

Did you know that Louis XIV, nicknamed the "Sun King," reigned over France for an incredible 72 years? Just imagine, it's like having the same president or prime minister since your grandparents were children! And he wasn't just any king, he was the center of everything, much like the sun in the middle of our solar system. Moreover, he had a gigantic castle built, the Palace of Versailles, where everyone had to follow him.

And then there was Elizabeth II, the Queen of England. She was like a super granny for the entire United Kingdom. She witnessed so many things, from musical trends to different presidents and prime ministers. Even though she is no longer with us, her legacy remains, solid as a rock.

Let's move on to a king who was a bit more... let's say, complicated. Henry VIII. This guy had a serious problem with marriage. He married six times because he absolutely wanted a son to be king after him. He even created his own Church so he could divorce whenever he wanted. Talk about drama!

Ah, and we must not forget Catherine the Great. She was Empress of Russia and did so much for her country. She was kind of like Russia's superhero of her time, except she didn't have a cape or superpowers, but a lot of intelligence and courage.

Do you like stories of ancient Egypt? Then you'll love Nefertiti. She was so beautiful that even today, thousands of years later, people are still fascinated by her face. She and her husband even tried to change all the beliefs of their country!

Philip II of Spain had such a large empire that it was said that "the sun never set" on it. Imagine having a garden so big that you never get to see the end of it!

Have you ever heard of Queen Victoria? She was Queen Elizabeth II's great-great-grandmother. She had an era named after her, the Victorian era, and her empire was the largest ever built. She loved her husband Albert so much that after his death, she spent the rest of her life in black to mourn him.

Charlemagne, what an impressive name, right? He was so strong and intelligent that he managed to unite almost all of Europe. It's a bit like someone managing to put together a giant puzzle all by themselves.

Cleopatra, the last queen of Egypt, was more than a beautiful woman. She was smart and brave. She loved her country so much that she did everything to save it, even if it meant having to seduce Roman emperors.

Richard the Lionheart, the crusading king, was so brave that he became a legend. You know, Robin Hood? Well, he was supposed to be one of Richard's friends.

Elizabeth I, Henry VIII's daughter, was a bit like the rock star of her time. She reigned over what is called the Golden Age in England. It was during her reign that guys like Shakespeare wrote plays that we still study in school today. And guess what? She even managed to thwart a huge fleet of Spanish ships that wanted to invade her country!

Then there's Akhenaten, an Egyptian pharaoh who decided to change all the rules. He said: "Stop! We're going to worship only one god now." It was super risky, and not everyone agreed, but he still tried. And he was the dad of Tutankhamun, you know, the pharaoh with the super famous mummy?

Louis XVI and Marie Antoinette, oh my, what a sad story! They were the last kings of France before everything collapsed during the French Revolution. They lived in luxury, while ordinary people barely had enough to eat. It didn't end very well for them, but their story shows us what can happen when leaders forget the people they are supposed to help.

The Queen of Sheba, known for her intelligence, traveled to Jerusalem to test King Solomon's wisdom with riddles and complex questions. Impressed by Solomon's insight, who was able to answer all her questions, she formed an alliance with him. This meeting became legendary, symbolizing a cultural and intellectual exchange between their kingdoms.

Edward the Confessor, one of the last Anglo-Saxon kings, had a super famous church built, Westminster Abbey. You know, it's where all the kings and queens of England have been crowned since.

Isabella I of Spain did something huge. She managed to drive the Moors out of Spain and unite the country. And she even paid for Christopher Columbus's voyage, which led to the discovery of America. Without her, who knows how things would have turned out?

Charles I of England had so many disputes with his advisors that they ended up having a civil war. And he lost. It's sad, but it shows us how important it is to get along with others when you're a leader.

Anne of Brittany was so popular that she was queen of France twice! First with Charles VIII, then with Louis XII. Thanks to her, Brittany became part of France.

Suleiman the Magnificent was really... magnificent! He was the Sultan of the Ottoman Empire and conquered a lot of territories. But he wasn't just a warrior, he also loved the arts and poetry.

And finally, Ramses II, a pharaoh who reigned for 66 years! He built gigantic monuments and some even say he met Moses, the one who parted the Red Sea in two.

Wonders of the World

Let's take a trip around the world to discover some of the most incredible constructions that have been made by people just like you and me, but a very, very long time ago!
Come on, put on your imaginary helmet for time and space travel purposes, and off we go!

Let's go back to Egypt. Did you know that the Great Pyramid of Giza is so large it would cover more than five football fields end to end? And the craziest part is that it was built without the help of modern machines! Thousands of workers used simple tools and a lot of muscle to move those huge blocks of stone.

Then, for the Hanging Gardens of Babylon, it seems they were built on several levels, like a giant birthday cake of plants and flowers! They might have even been watered using an ingenious technique that brought water from the nearby river.

For the statue of Zeus in Greece, it was so large and impressive that those who saw it felt tiny in comparison. The sculptor Phidias used gold and ivory to decorate it. Just imagine, a giant shiny god welcoming you!

In Ephesus, the Temple of Artemis was so fabulous that people came from far away to admire it. The temple had 127 columns, each 18 meters high! That's almost as tall as six giraffes stacked on top of each other!

In Petra, Jordan, the city was carved into pink rock. Imagine artisans carving castles and temples directly into the stone! And all this in a canyon in the middle of the desert!

For the Iguazu Falls, they are so large that they could fill nearly 500,000 swimming pools in a single day! It's as if the water is dancing and jumping from rock to rock, creating an incredible natural spectacle.

Machu Picchu, located in the Andes mountains of Peru at a dizzying altitude of nearly 2,430 meters. Imagine climbing a mountain and finding an entire city at the top, with temples, fountains, and even a farm!

The Taj Mahal in India is not just a pretty building. It's a monument to love! Emperor Shah Jahan had it built in honor of his beloved wife. The white marble is so pure that it seems to change color with the daylight. In the morning, it can be pink and in the evening, golden!

Hạ Long Bay in Vietnam is like a postcard landscape but in real life. Imagine yourself on a boat, navigating between thousands of islands and rocky islets emerging from the water like sleeping dragons. It's a dream for budding adventurers!

The Colosseum in Rome, Italy, is more than just a stadium. It was the theater of gladiator fights, naval clashes, and even battles with real wild animals! This place could accommodate 50,000 people, it's like a football stadium, but for Roman-era fights!

Chichén Itzá in Mexico is famous for its large pyramid. But that's not all! There is also a playing field for an ancient sport that was a bit like basketball, except that if you lost, the consequences could be really serious. It is even thought that the players risked their lives!

The City of the Sky in Teotihuacan is fascinating. Imagine an ancient city with pyramids as tall as 20-story buildings! The people who lived there were so advanced that they even had sewage systems.

The Statue of Liberty in New York is a true symbol of freedom and welcome. It measures nearly 46 meters from the base to the tip of the torch. And did you know that it was sent by boat from France in 350 pieces? It's like a gigantic construction set!

The Panama Canal is an engineering feat. It took 10 years and more than 75,000 workers to build it. Thanks to this canal, ships no longer have to make the long detour around South America, which is a significant saving of time!

Pirates and Their Hidden Treasures

Blackbeard, whose real name was Edward Teach, was a terrifying pirate. He would tie lit fuses into his beard to look even more frightening. Just imagine seeing this pirate with flames in his beard boarding your ship!

La Buse's treasure is one of the greatest mysteries of piracy. This treasure has never been found, but some say it would contain mountains of gold and precious stones. A real treasure worthy of an adventure movie!

Anne Bonny and Mary Read were two formidable female pirates. They were not only brave, they were also very skilled with a sword. They prove that piracy wasn't just a man's business.

The "Whydah Gally" was a pirate ship that sank with a huge cargo of gold and silver. This treasure was discovered centuries later and contained more than 200,000 artifacts!

Calico Jack was famous for his pirate flag with a skull and crossed sabers. It's thanks to him that this symbol has become the universal logo of pirates.

The legend of Libertalia is fascinating. Imagine an island ruled by pirates, where everyone is free and equal. It sounds like a fairy tale for sea brigands!

Captain Kidd was such a famous pirate that he was even tried and hanged in London. Legends say that he buried treasures all over the place, and treasure hunters are still looking for them today.

The treasure of Cocos Island is another mystery that makes adventurers dream. Some say that this treasure would be so large that it could never be transported by a single person.

Port Royal in Jamaica was like the great capital of pirates. Imagine a city where pirates are kings and queens, with treasures on every street corner!

The "Golden Hind" was the first English ship to circumnavigate the globe. Sir Francis Drake, its captain, returned to England with so much gold and silver that Queen Elizabeth I herself came to see it.

The treasure of the "Flor de la Mar" is another treasure lost at sea. This Portuguese ship sank with so much gold and precious stones that no one has ever been able to estimate its value.

Bartholomew Roberts, or "Black Bart," was a very successful pirate. He captured over 400 ships, making him the most "successful" pirate in history.

The "Atocha" was a Spanish treasure ship that sank in Florida. The treasure was found in 1985 and contained tons of gold, silver, and precious stones.

The Pirate Republic in Nassau was another paradise for pirates. It was like a holiday club for outlaws, where they could rest between two looting sessions.

Captain Morgan was not only a formidable pirate but also a fine strategist. And yes, he gave his name to the famous rum!

The "San José" was a Spanish galleon filled with treasures that sank in 1708. It was discovered in 2015 near Colombia, and its treasure is estimated at several billion dollars.

Flibustiers and Boucaniers were different types of pirates. Flibustiers were often French, while boucaniers were initially hunters.

The "Jolly Roger" is the name of the pirate flag with a skull and crossbones. This flag was raised just before the attack to spread terror.

The Pirate Code was like the rules of the game for pirates. This code dictated how to share the loot, treat prisoners, and resolve disputes.

Edward Low was known for his cruelty. He did not hesitate to torture and kill those who stood in his way. His flag showed a red skeleton, a sign of his violent nature.

Festivals and Traditions of the World

Blackbeard, whose real name was Edward Teach, was a terrifying pirate. He would tie lit fuses into his beard to look even more frightening. Just imagine seeing this pirate with flames in his beard boarding your ship!

La Buse's treasure is one of the greatest mysteries of piracy. This treasure has never been found, but some say it would contain mountains of gold and precious stones. A real treasure worthy of an adventure movie!

Anne Bonny and Mary Read were two formidable female pirates. They were not only brave, they were also very skilled with a sword. They prove that piracy wasn't just a man's business.

The "Whydah Gally" was a pirate ship that sank with a huge cargo of gold and silver. This treasure was discovered centuries later and contained more than 200,000 artifacts!

Calico Jack was famous for his pirate flag with a skull and crossed sabers. It's thanks to him that this symbol has become the universal logo of pirates.

The legend of Libertalia is fascinating. Imagine an island ruled by pirates, where everyone is free and equal. It sounds like a fairy tale for sea brigands!

Captain Kidd was such a famous pirate that he was even tried and hanged in London. Legends say that he buried treasures all over the place, and treasure hunters are still looking for them today.

The treasure of Cocos Island is another mystery that makes adventurers dream. Some say that this treasure would be so large that it could never be transported by a single person.

Port Royal in Jamaica was like the great capital of pirates. Imagine a city where pirates are kings and queens, with treasures on every street corner!

The "Golden Hind" was the first English ship to circumnavigate the globe. Sir Francis Drake, its captain, returned to England with so much gold and silver that Queen Elizabeth I herself came to see it.

The treasure of the "Flor de la Mar" is another treasure lost at sea. This Portuguese ship sank with so much gold and precious stones that no one has ever been able to estimate its value.

Bartholomew Roberts, or "Black Bart," was a very successful pirate. He captured over 400 ships, making him the most "successful" pirate in history.

The "Atocha" was a Spanish treasure ship that sank in Florida. The treasure was found in 1985 and contained tons of gold, silver, and precious stones.

The Pirate Republic in Nassau was another paradise for pirates. It was like a holiday club for outlaws, where they could rest between two looting sessions.

Captain Morgan was not only a formidable pirate but also a fine strategist. And yes, he gave his name to the famous rum!

The "San José" was a Spanish galleon filled with treasures that sank in 1708. It was discovered in 2015 near Colombia, and its treasure is estimated at several billion dollars.

Flibustiers and Boucaniers were different types of pirates. Flibustiers were often French, while boucaniers were initially hunters.

The "Jolly Roger" is the name of the pirate flag with a skull and crossbones. This flag was raised just before the attack to spread terror.

The Pirate Code was like the rules of the game for pirates. This code dictated how to share the loot, treat prisoners, and resolve disputes.

Edward Low was known for his cruelty. He did not hesitate to torture and kill those who stood in his way. His flag showed a red skeleton, a sign of his violent nature.

Superfoods and Nutrition

Goji berries, originating from the Himalayan mountains, are like little pearls of energy. They are packed with antioxidants and vitamins that give you a boost.

Quinoa, often called "the gold of the Incas," is a seed that acts like a grain. High in protein and essential amino acids, it's a staple in vegetarian diets.

Chia seeds are small, but their impact on health is huge. They are filled with omega-3s that are good for the heart and aid digestion.

Kale, this dark green leafy vegetable, is a real nutritional treasure. It is so rich in vitamins and minerals that some consider it one of the healthiest foods on the planet.

Turmeric, this orange-yellow spice, is known for its anti-inflammatory properties. It's often used in Indian cooking and detox drinks.

Açaí berries come from the Amazon rainforest and are a true antioxidant bomb. They help fight free radicals that cause aging.

Spinach was Popeye's favorite food for good reason. It's rich in iron and calcium, making it excellent for bone and muscle health.

Nuts are tasty and nutritious little snacks. They are full of good fats and proteins that help you stay energetic throughout the day.

Avocado is like the king of healthy fats. Not only is it delicious in guacamole or on toast, but it also helps with the absorption of nutrients from other foods.

Moringa, often called the "miracle tree," is used in traditional medicine for its many virtues. Its leaves are a concentration of nutrients: protein, calcium, potassium, and vitamins.

Green tea is like a magic potion for your body. It boosts metabolism, aids in weight loss, and is filled with antioxidants.

Ginger is an excellent natural remedy for a multitude of ailments. It is particularly effective in soothing nausea and strengthening the immune system.

Flaxseeds are small but mighty. They are a rich source of omega-3 and fiber, making them excellent for digestion and heart health.

Garlic is more than just a flavoring for your cooking. It's a powerful antimicrobial and can help reduce blood pressure.

The sweet potato, with its beautiful orange color, is rich in beta-carotene, which is excellent for eye health.

Blueberries are like little antioxidant bombs. They are so rich in nutrients that you'll feel like a superhero after eating them.

Whole grains are allies for your digestive system. They are rich in fiber and help reduce the risk of heart disease.

Black beans are a great way to add protein to your diet, especially if you're vegetarian. They are also rich in fiber.

Salmon is a fatty fish that is a fantastic source of omega-3. Not only is it good for the heart, but it's also great for the brain.

Broccoli is the all-rounder vegetable. Rich in vitamins and antioxidants, it's an excellent addition to any meal.

World Records

Ah, world records! They remind us of how extraordinary human beings can be. Take Lee Redmond, for example. Imagine having nails that reach a total length of 8.65 meters. Doing the dishes must be quite a challenge!

And let's talk about Lucky Diamond Rich, the world's most tattooed man. He even has tattoos inside his ears and on his eyelids. One can say he is truly dedicated to his body art.

Courage is also celebrated. AJ Hackett bungee jumped from the top of the Macau Tower, at a dizzying height of 233 meters. A jump that surely made his heart race!

As for Robert Wadlow, the tallest man documented in history, he stood an incredible 2.72 meters without shoes. One can only imagine the daily challenges he faced.

Jeanne Calment, a French woman, holds the record for the oldest person, having lived up to 122 years and 164 days. She witnessed the birth and growth of several generations and many historical events.

Italy, the land of pizza, did not disappoint by creating the world's largest pizza, with an area of 1,261.65 m². That's a lot of cheese and tomato sauce!

In 1952, a couple danced non-stop for more than 35 hours. Their feet must have been exhausted, but what endurance!

The Cullinan, the largest diamond ever found, weighed 3,106.75 carats. It was divided into several precious stones, some of which adorn the British crown.

Ram Singh Chauhan, for his part, can boast of having the world's longest mustache, measuring 4.29 meters. One can imagine it must take him some time to style it each morning.

And who would have thought that a TV show in Norway could last 217 hours live? That's almost ten days of continuous broadcasting!

Of course, the list of records is still long and just as fascinating. Take the example of the cake that held the most candles: 72,585 to be precise. It must have been an incredible light show, and one can only hope that no fires were started!

And what about Barivel, this Maine Coon who holds the record for the world's longest cat? Measuring 120 cm from head to tail, this feline is almost as long as a child!

Meanwhile, in China, a team created a gigantic ice sculpture of 52,234.56 m³ in 2010. Imagine the talent and precision needed to sculpt a work of art of this magnitude!

Imelda Marcos, the former First Lady of the Philippines, was a shoe collector with more than 3,000 pairs. A true fashion temple, albeit controversial.

Adrienn Banhegyi skipped rope 377 times in just 60 seconds, proving that a minute can be very long if you know how to use it.

Lai Chi-wai, for his part, climbed 250 steps by pushing his wheelchair with his head. A feat that not only defies gravity but also human limits.

If you thought putting curlers was a quick task, think about the person who put 526 curlers in an hour. That must be a hard record to beat!

A Thai couple shared the longest kiss ever recorded, lasting 58 hours, 35 minutes, and 58 seconds. One wonders how they managed to eat or drink during all that time!

In the United States, the heaviest sandwich weighed 2,467.5 kg and was prepared at Wild Woody's Chill and Grill. That's a lot of bread, lettuce, and meat!

In the Maldives, 308 divers formed the longest human chain underwater in 2019. A beautiful demonstration of coordination and unity.

Records continue to surprise us and push the boundaries of what we thought possible. Like those people who gathered to form the world's largest zombie dance, in tribute to Michael Jackson's famous video "Thriller". Imagine hundreds of people dressed as zombies, dancing in perfect synchronization!

Or the record for the most people playing chess simultaneously. In a gigantic hall, hundreds of chess tables were lined up, each player focused on their own game while being part of a collective feat.

Ashrita Furman holds an impressive record: he traveled 123.45 meters balanced on a giant circus ball. His feat took place on November 17, 2004, in Belize. Each step had to be carefully calculated to maintain his balance on this round and unstable surface.

French chef Michel Lotito holds the record for the most pancakes made in one hour, preparing 1,127 pancakes. This means he flipped almost one pancake every three seconds, an impressive performance of speed and dexterity.

Mario Morby, a passionate Briton, holds the record for the largest collection of postcards, with more than 1.5 million pieces. His collection, which covers the walls of his house, is like a journey through the world and history, each postcard telling a different story from a place or time. It's a visual treasure representing diverse cultures and historical moments captured on small pieces of cardboard.

The record for the largest gathering of people dressed as superheroes was set in 2010 when 1,580 participants gathered in Australia, wearing the capes and costumes of their favorite heroes. It was a colorful spectacle where Batman, Superman, Wonder Woman, and many others mingled, creating a scene worthy of a superhero movie.

As for Ashrita Furman, he is the undisputed king of Guinness World Records. With over 600 records set, he has turned the achievement of the extraordinary into a daily routine. Whether juggling apples while eating them or skipping rope during a marathon, Furman continues to push the boundaries of human endurance and determination.

Or consider the record for the most balloons burst by a dog in less than 60 seconds. Yes, you heard right, it's a record held by a dog named "Cally the Wonderdog". This little animal managed to burst 100 balloons in just 42.4 seconds, proving that world records are not just for humans.

And what about Dinesh Shivnath Upadhyaya, who managed to put 88 grapes in his mouth in one minute? A feat that requires not only a large mouth but also incredible dexterity and coordination.

The example of the largest domino assembly, composed of 277,275 pieces, shows how important teamwork and precision are. The final spectacle, when all the dominos collapse in perfect sequence, is breathtaking.

Or, the record for the most selfies taken in one hour. This record was set by Dwayne "The Rock" Johnson with 105 selfies, proving that even celebrities can enter the record books for rather unexpected feats.

The record for the largest drawing made by a robot was set in 2021 by a group of engineers in Italy. The robot, named "DAVINCI", drew a gigantic image of a girl on a surface of 6,118.62 square meters, using a specialized pen.

And let's not forget the record for the largest fireworks waterfall, where 70,000 rockets were launched in a span of less than 30 seconds, lighting up the night sky like never before.

Legendary Athletes

Imagine Jesse Owens, feet firmly planted on the track at the 1936 Berlin Olympics. Winning four gold medals, he did more than run; he openly defied the racist ideologies of the Nazi regime, overturning them with every stride.

Then, consider Michael Jordan. After being cut from his high school basketball team, he turned that failure into fuel for his determination, climbing the ranks to become the greatest basketball player of all time. A true phoenix rising from the ashes.

And what about Pelé? At an age when most teenagers are still learning the ropes of soccer, he dazzled the world by becoming the youngest player to score in a World Cup at just 17 years old.

Muhammad Ali, meanwhile, taught us that the fight isn't limited to the ring. With his famous phrase "Float like a butterfly, sting like a bee," he dodged military service during the Vietnam War, guided by his deep religious convictions.

Wilma Rudolph overcame adversity from an early age. After battling polio, she became the first American woman to win three gold medals in athletics at a single Olympiad.

Roger Bannister, on the other hand, defied the unimaginable. In 1954, he broke the psychological and physical barrier of the mile in under 4 minutes, a feat many considered impossible.

In gymnastics, Nadia Comăneci achieved perfection, literally. At the 1976 Olympics, she scored the first perfect 10, forever changing the face of her sport.

Usain Bolt, nicknamed "Lightning," shattered the world record for the 100 meters with a breathtaking time of 9.58 seconds. A performance that almost defies human understanding.

Serena Williams showed the strength and resilience of female athletes by winning a Grand Slam tournament while pregnant. A true feat that expanded the horizons of the possible.

Jackie Robinson forever changed the face of baseball by becoming the first African American to play in MLB (Major League Baseball) in 1947, thus breaking the racial barrier in a once-segregated sport.

Michele Mouton was not only one of the most successful female rally drivers, but she also co-founded the "Race of Champions" in memory of her deceased driver friend. A dual achievement that testifies to her talent and compassion.

Lionel Messi, despite a growth hormone deficiency during his childhood, overcame this obstacle to become one of the greatest soccer players of all time. A true story of perseverance and triumph over adversity.

Billie Jean King, a tennis legend, played a crucial role in the fight for gender equality in sports. In 1973, she won the "Battle of the Sexes," a highly publicized match against Bobby Riggs, thus affirming the competence and strength of female athletes.

Michael Phelps, this extraordinary swimmer, has a record that speaks for itself. He holds the record for the most Olympic gold medals, with an impressive total of 23 titles. A feat that places him in the pantheon of Olympic athletes.

Simone Biles, with her revolutionary moves, has completely changed the dynamics of gymnastics. Not only is she an incredibly gifted athlete, but she is also considered one of the greatest gymnasts of all time.

Arnold Schwarzenegger, long before becoming a film icon and politician, was a renowned bodybuilder. He won the Mr. Olympia title seven times, setting a standard for bodybuilding that endures to this day.

Althea Gibson broke barriers by becoming the first black player to win a Grand Slam tennis title in 1956. A pioneer who paved the way for generations of diverse talent in sports.

Kobe Bryant left an indelible mark on the world of basketball. Notably, he scored 81 points in an NBA game in 2006, the second-highest point total in a single game in league history.

Rafael Nadal, the "King of Clay," has an unmatched dominance on the Roland-Garros court with 13 titles to his name. A reign that defies all competition and makes him one of the greatest tennis players of all time.

Fanny Blankers-Koen, nicknamed "The Flying Mother," was much more than an extraordinary athlete. She won four gold medals in athletics at the 1948 Olympics while being a mother of two. A shining example that proves personal challenges are not a barrier to excellence.

Great Animal Migrations

Arctic caribou undertake an annual monumental journey of nearly 1,500 km, one of the longest terrestrial migrations made by a mammal. Their trek across mountains, rivers, and snowy plains is an eloquent testament to their endurance and survival instinct.

Let's talk about monarch butterflies. These delicate creatures travel up to 4,500 km during their migration from Canada to Mexico. Their journey is so extraordinary that it requires several generations to complete. A true aerial relay orchestrated by nature!

Humpback whales, these majestic giants of the seas, undertake an annual migration of 25,000 km. They leave the cold polar waters for warmer tropical waters where they give birth to their offspring. A monumental displacement for new life.

The wildebeests of the Serengeti in Tanzania, accompanied by zebras and antelopes, undertake a circular migration of nearly

3,000 km each year. This collective cavalcade is an unceasing quest for fresh grass and new horizons.

Pacific salmon return to their birthplace to reproduce after spending several years at sea. To do this, they swim up rivers for hundreds of kilometers, braving both currents and predators. A migration that is a true epic of life and death.

Bats from Bracken Cave in Texas form the world's largest gathering of mammals. Millions of individuals leave their cave each summer to migrate to Mexico, a natural spectacle that commands admiration.

Emperor penguins, true heroes of Antarctica, sometimes walk up to 120 km to reach their breeding sites. These birds are the only ones to breed during the Antarctic winter, defying extremely freezing temperatures.

Sea turtles live a fascinating aquatic adventure. Born on beaches, they embark on a journey across the oceans of our planet. When it's time to lay their eggs, they often return to the same beach where they were born, a life cycle that is a true marine odyssey.

Small Arctic birds like the sanderling undertake a migratory flight that takes them from the Arctic to Antarctica. These valiant little birds travel almost 32,000 km each year, a distance that underscores their incredible endurance.

As for African elephants, these land giants are known for their long migrations in search of water and food. Their spatial memory is so developed that they can find water points after long periods, even over hundreds of kilometers.

Dragonflies, despite their small size, are no less impressive. Some species travel up to 7,000 km between India and Africa, crossing oceans and deserts. A feat that reminds us that size is not always synonymous with limits.

Gray whales, these other titans of the oceans, perform one of the longest migrations of all marine mammals. Their journey extends over approximately 20,000 km, from the cold waters of the Arctic to the warm lagoons of Mexico, where they find refuge to reproduce.

Albatrosses, with their majestic wings, are experts in long-distance flight. They can travel up to 10,000 km without landing, soaring over the vast ocean expanses of our planet.

Reindeer, robust inhabitants of the Arctic regions, travel up to 5,000 km a year to access new pastures. Their migration is a true crossing of rivers and mountains, a large-scale terrestrial adventure.

Flamingos, these birds with distinctive pink plumage, travel long distances to find ideal habitats for feeding and breeding. Some of them travel more than 2,000 km, connecting wetlands in Africa and Asia.

Flying lizards, despite their misleading name, are great migrants. They can glide over 800 km to find feeding or breeding areas, an astonishing ability for a reptile.

Martial Arts of the World

Karate, this ancient discipline from Okinawa in Japan, carries in its very name its philosophy: "empty hand". Beyond striking with hands and feet, this martial art teaches a rigorous discipline, almost meditative.

Capoeira, a combat dance born in Brazil, is as much a form of artistic expression as it is a martial art. Developed by African slaves, it is distinguished by its acrobatic movements and enchanting rhythms, a true spectacle for the senses.

Taekwondo, a proud representative of Korean culture, literally translates to "the way of the foot and the fist". With its jumping and spinning kicks, it is much more than just a sport; it's a school of life teaching respect and courtesy.

Kung-fu, this rich and diverse Chinese martial art, encompasses a multitude of styles, each with its own specificities. Often associated with meditation and the management of "qi", or vital energy, it is a complete art.

Judo, born in Japan, is a "way of flexibility" that relies on throws and ground holds. But beyond techniques, it teaches essential values such as self-control and respect for the opponent.

Aikido, also Japanese, is an art of fluidity. Rather than directly opposing the opponent's force, it aims to redirect it, to use it against him in a dance of circular movements.

Muay Thai, Thailand's national sport, is often called "the art of eight limbs". Using fists, elbows, knees, and shins, it is both a brutal and elegant combat system.

Silat, coming from the Malay and Indonesian regions, is a graceful yet formidable martial art. The movements, often performed in harmony with traditional music, conceal effective self-defense techniques.

Sambo, this Russian martial art, is a hybrid mix of judo and wrestling. Originally designed for military combat, it specializes in ground holds and submission techniques.

Krav Maga, originating in Israel, is a pragmatic response to modern threats. Focused on self-defense, it teaches how to react quickly and effectively to various dangerous situations.

Brazilian jiu-jitsu, which has its roots in judo, has developed into a unique form of martial art in Brazil. Specializing in ground combat, it offers a strategy where even the weakest can triumph through elaborate submission techniques.

French boxing, or "savate", skillfully blends kicks and punches. What sets it apart are its special shoes, "savate shoes", which are an integral part of this elegant yet formidable martial art.

Wing Chun, a particular style of kung-fu, is an ode to speed and precision. This martial art is famous for its "wooden dummy", a unique training tool that helps perfect striking and blocking techniques.

Kali, also known as eskrima or arnis, is a Philippine martial art focused on weapon handling. Whether it's sticks, knives, or even bare hands, this art is a veritable arsenal of combat techniques.

Kyudo, which means "the way of the bow" in Japanese, is the traditional art of archery. More than just a shooting skill, it aims to achieve a form of inner perfection, in harmony with the gesture of the bow and arrow.

Lucha libre, a Mexican variant of professional wrestling, is a colorful spectacle. Known for its vibrant masks and aerial acrobatics, it is a true cultural phenomenon beyond its sporting aspect.

Sumo is more than a wrestling sport; it's an ancient Japanese ritual. Two giants face off in a sacred circle, and the goal is not only to bring down the opponent but also to win with dignity.

Ninjutsu, the art of shadows, is often associated with ninjas, the legendary spies and assassins of feudal Japan. Beyond combat techniques, it includes elements of strategy, stealth, and even psychological manipulation.

Hapkido, from Korea, is a versatile martial art that mixes kicks, holds, and weapon techniques. It offers a hybrid approach to combat, combining various elements to create a complete self-defense system.

Tai Chi, often associated with a form of moving meditation, is also a full-fledged Chinese martial art. Its slow and fluid movements hide combat techniques that are not only beautiful to watch but also incredibly effective.

Space Travel and Space Conquest

1961 was marked by a breathtaking achievement: Yuri Gagarin, aboard the Vostok 1 capsule, became the first human to float in the vastness of space, completing a full orbit around the Earth.

Then in 1969, the Apollo 11 mission etched its name in the annals of history. Neil Armstrong and Buzz Aldrin walked on the Moon, an achievement that made millions of hearts on our blue planet throb.

The International Space Station, launched in 1998, is a marvel of engineering and diplomacy. It symbolizes international cooperation in the quest for space knowledge.

Who could forget the sumptuous images from the Hubble Space Telescope? Since its launch in 1990, it has revolutionized our perception of the universe, revealing distant galaxies and dazzling nebulae.

The Rosetta probe, launched in 2004, provided a thrilling moment in 2014 when its lander, Philae, touched down on comet 67P, a first in the history of space exploration.

The red planet, Mars, fascinates and intrigues. Rovers like Curiosity and Perseverance comb its arid soil in search of signs of water and ancient life.

The Space Shuttle, which flew between 1981 and 2011, was the workhorse of space exploration, making multiple missions possible, including the construction of the ISS (International Space Station).

SpaceX's Crew Dragon mission in 2020 opened a new chapter by becoming the first commercial mission to send astronauts to the ISS.

The Voyager 1 and 2 probes, launched more than 40 years ago in 1977, are true space pioneers and continue to send us data from the edges of the solar system and beyond.

NASA's Artemis project is highly ambitious, aiming to return humans to the Moon by 2024, but this time with the intention of staying there.

The Sun is not being neglected. The Parker Solar Probe ventures closer than ever to unlock the secrets of our star.

The asteroid belt, that field of rocks between Mars and Jupiter, also attracts attention. The OSIRIS-REx mission aims to collect samples from the asteroid Bennu.

Black holes, those cosmic enigmas, are now less mysterious thanks to the Event Horizon Telescope, which captured the first image of a black hole in 2019.

SpaceX's Starship project aims for nothing less than the colonization of Mars. An ambitious project that could redefine the future of humanity.

In the search for worlds beyond our own, telescopes like Kepler scan the skies, revealing the existence of potentially habitable exoplanets.

China is not to be outdone with its successful lunar missions, especially Chang'e 5, which brought back samples from the Moon in 2020.

The James Webb Space Telescope, awaiting its launch, is expected to revolutionize our understanding of the universe.

Companies like Blue Origin and Virgin Galactic are working on space tourism, an idea once confined to science fiction novels.

Asteroid mining is another burgeoning field. These space rocks could be the gold mines of the future.

Magicians and Illusionists

Harry Houdini, that prodigy of escape, captivated the collective imagination well beyond his time. Artistically nicknamed the great escape artist, he fascinated the world with his performances. Chained and submerged underwater or locked in his terrifying "Chinese Water Torture Cell", he escaped from inextricable situations, defying the laws of physics and human logic. His feats, such as the "Metamorphosis" and his escapes from locked boxes, largely contributed to his mysterious aura.

Since the 1920s, the "sawing a woman in half" trick has captivated audiences. This trick, using the art of misdirection and secret compartments, creates a disconcerting illusion that continues to fascinate by its ability to play with a visceral fear while reassuring with a happy conclusion.

David Copperfield, the maestro of illusion, has redefined the boundaries of magic with spectacular acts such as the disappearance of the Statue of Liberty in 1983. His audacity and imagination have transformed iconic locations into mere actors in his astonishing performances.

Derren Brown, the British mentalist, combines suggestion and psychology to deceive and amaze his audience. His tricks, exploring the confines of psychology, create illusions so convincing that they call into question the reliability of our own senses.

The illusion of levitation and the "torture chamber" trick are classics of magic that use transparent wires, hidden platforms, and frames of sharp spikes respectively to create illusions of weightlessness and perilous escape.

"Palmage" is a subtle but effective technique. The magician, hiding objects in the palm of his hand, deceives even the most attentive spectators, proof that in the art of illusion, every detail counts.

Contemporary artists like Dynamo and Criss Angel have pushed the boundaries of what we consider possible, "walking" on the Thames or on the water of a pool, feats that seem to defy the laws of nature itself.

The "guillotine trick" and "misdirection" play with the fears and attention of the audience. Thanks to fake knives, rigged heads, and the art of diverting attention, these tricks prove that every gesture has meaning and every second is an opportunity for illusion.

Penn & Teller, the American duo, break the mold by revealing the secrets of some tricks while performing illusions that leave the audience speechless, representing a meta-magic that plays with our expectations.

Coin magic and the "flying ring trick" require incredible dexterity. These tricks, where objects disappear and reappear unexpectedly, are perfect examples of interactive magic.

David Blaine, known for his street magic and endurance stunts, has performed feats like being buried alive for several days, while Teller, of the Penn & Teller duo, is famous for his silent performance, using gestures and expressions to perform tricks without a word.

Robert-Houdin, often cited as the father of modern magic, used electromagnetism to perform some of his most astonishing tricks, showing that magic is also about understanding and using science to one's advantage.

In conclusion, magic is an art of illusion that relies on a combination of dexterity, psychology, technology, and storytelling. Whether through classic tricks or modern feats, magicians continue to challenge our perception of reality, reminding us that the world is still full of mystery and wonder.

The Age of Dinosaurs

About 230 million years ago, during the geological period known as the Triassic, our Earth witnessed the emergence of the first dinosaurs. These extraordinary creatures dominated our planet for millions of years, leaving an indelible mark on the ecosystem.

Among them, the Tyrannosaurus rex, a colossus about 12 meters long, terrorized its prey. Its impressive stature did not prevent it from reaching surprising speeds of up to 20 km/h, making it a formidable predator and a conductor in the ecosystem of its time, a delicate balance between predation and survival.

The sauropods, such as Brachiosaurus, were true terrestrial giants. Some specimens reached up to 26 meters in length. Their enormous size and long neck, allowing them to reach high leaves, is a feat of biology, defying our understanding of animal anatomy, while playing a crucial role in regulating vegetation.

However, not all dinosaurs were giants. The Compsognathus, for example, was the size of a chicken. This variety of sizes testifies to the great diversity of these prehistoric creatures, where even the smallest had their role to play, contributing to the balance of their habitat.

Some dinosaurs, like the Velociraptor, had feathers. Although most of these dinosaurs were not capable of flight, their presence suggests an evolutionary transition towards birds, adding an additional layer of complexity to our understanding of these fascinating animals.

The Stegosaurus, with its dorsal plates and caudal spikes, lived during the Jurassic period, about 150 million years ago. Its distinct morphology makes it a work of art of nature, each element of its anatomy contributing to its survival in a dangerous world.

During the era of dinosaurs, the first birds like Archaeopteryx appeared. This evolutionary turning point, marked by the transition from crawling to flying, shows how astonishing the diversity of life can be and how these creatures were able to conquer new horizons.

Triceratops, with their three horns and a large cranial shield, were herbivores adapted to defend against predators like T. rex. Their imposing cranial shield and horns probably made them the prehistoric equivalent of a vegetarian tank.

The Spinosaurus, with its impressive dorsal sail, was another large carnivore, even surpassing T. rex in size. This unique dinosaur, a giant among giants, enriches our understanding of the diversity of prehistoric life forms. Its dorsal sail and immense size distinguish it as another prodigy of evolution.

During the Cretaceous period, the emergence of flowers added color and diversity to a world already rich in life forms. The relationships between these plants and herbivorous dinosaurs were probably complex, creating new food chains and complex ecological relationships.

The era of dinosaurs came to an end about 65 million years ago, in a cataclysm likely caused by an asteroid impact, a mass extinction event that ended the domination of these creatures on Earth. This dark but essential chapter in their saga reminds us of the fragility of life and the potential impact of large-scale environmental changes.

World Music and Dances

Salsa, the intoxicating blend of African rhythms and Spanish instruments, was born in Cuba. This energetic dance is an explosion of movement and color, making it a joyful expression of Caribbean culture.

K-pop, the cultural wave from South Korea, has conquered the world with its fusion of pop, rap, and sometimes rock. The performances are often spectacular, showcasing precise choreographies that captivate fans worldwide.

In India, Bharatanatyam holds a sacred place among classical dances. This ancient dance narrates stories through graceful movements and facial expressions, establishing a deep connection between art and spirituality.

Andalusia, Spain, is the birthplace of Flamenco. This dance is an explosion of emotions, combining singing, dancing, and guitar playing in an intense and captivating artistic performance.

In Argentina, the tango is much more than a dance; it's a love story set in motion. The music, often played with a bandoneon, adds a layer of passion to this already intense dance.

Reggae, the iconic musical genre from Jamaica, is an anthem to relaxation and love. Its slow and steady rhythm offers a striking contrast to the speed and energy of many other popular dances.

Samba is the soul of Rio's Carnival in Brazil. This fast and joyful dance is a true visual spectacle, with dancers dressed in dazzling and colorful costumes parading to the rhythm of the music.

Egyptian Baladi is a traditional folk dance often performed with an ornate belt that accentuates the fluid body movements. It's a celebration of Egyptian culture and history.

In Ireland, tap dancing is a display of skill and rhythm. The special shoes used amplify each movement, making the performance even more impressive.

Hip-hop, born in the inner-city neighborhoods of New York, is more than a dance; it's a means of social expression. The rhythmic movements are often performed to rap music, giving a voice to marginalized communities.

In Russia, the Kalinka dance is a display of joy and energy, known for its jumps and rapid squats. It is often accompanied by cheerful singing, adding a cultural dimension to the performance.

Japanese Taiko is a percussive experience that goes beyond mere music. The drums are played with choreographed and powerful movements, creating a performance that is visually and auditorily captivating.

Hawaiian Hula is a dance that tells stories through graceful hand movements and swaying hips. Often accompanied by chanting, it's a true narrative art in motion.

Belly dancing, or oriental dance, is a celebration of femininity and sensuality, highlighting the fluid movements of the torso and hips.

Jazz, this complex and varied musical genre originating from the United States, is also associated with improvised dance movements, giving each performance a unique character.

The polka, this joyful dance from Central Europe, is often accompanied by an accordion, adding a festive layer to the performance.

In Indonesia, gamelan is a traditional musical ensemble consisting mainly of percussion. It often accompanies dances or ceremonies, adding cultural depth to each event.

Traditional African dances vary greatly from one region to another. However, they are often rhythmic and vigorous, playing a central role in celebrations and community rites.

Rock 'n' roll, with its energetic dance moves like the "twist," revolutionized music and dance in the 1950s. It remains a symbol of an era of change and freedom.

The waltz, this elegant and flowing European dance, is often the star of formal balls. Its three-time music creates an atmosphere of romance and refinement.

Inventors and Their Creations

Thomas Edison is often reduced to the invention of the light bulb, but this ingenious mind also gave birth to the phonograph, an incredible machine that allowed sound to be recorded and played back for the first time.

Alexander Graham Bell, the man behind the telephone, wasn't just a one-idea inventor. He also worked to help deaf people, showing a variety of interests and a desire to make the world better.

Before John Gorrie's invention of the refrigerator, food preservation was a chilly affair, literally! People used ice and more primitive preservation methods to keep their food cool.

Can you imagine a world without safe elevators? Thanks to Elisha Otis, who in 1852 introduced a safety mechanism that revolutionized vertical transportation in buildings.

Kites, those celestial objects of our childhood, come to us from ancient China. They were invented more than 2000 years ago and have crossed the centuries to brighten our modern skies.

George Eastman democratized photography by inventing roll film. This invention led to the creation of Kodak and made capturing precious moments accessible to everyone.

Imagine a world where you struggle to see clearly: difficult, isn't it? Glasses, invented in the 13th century in Italy, have come to the rescue of millions of people throughout the ages.

The first concept of a computer is attributed to Charles Babbage and his Analytical Engine in 1837. Although it was never fully realized, this idea laid the groundwork for modern computing.

Douglas Engelbart invented the computer mouse in 1964, thus facilitating interaction with these still-new machines. This tool has become so common that we can no longer imagine our digital life without it.

The ballpoint pen, this everyday object, was invented by Laszlo Biro in 1938. It ended the era of fountain pens and spilled ink, simplifying writing for generations.

The fan, both a practical and elegant accessory, is another gift from ancient China. It was used to cool off but also acquired aesthetic and social value.

Marie Curie is an icon of science. She not only discovered radium but is also the only person to have won Nobel Prizes in two different scientific disciplines.

The first vacuum cleaner was so large that it required a cart to transport it. Thanks to Hubert Cecil Booth for this invention in 1901 that changed our way of cleaning.

Velcro, this practical invention, was inspired by nature. George de Mestral had this idea in 1941 after a walk where burdock seeds stuck to his clothes.

The Slinky, a toy that walks down stairs on its own, was born by accident. Richard James was inspired when he saw a spring fall and "walk," giving birth to this classic toy.

Umbrellas have a sunny history! Originally, they were used for sun protection in ancient Egypt and were a sign of social status.

Scissors, these essential tools, were invented in Egypt more than 3000 years ago. An ancient invention but still relevant today.

The video game Pong paved the way for the video game era. Released in 1972, this simple but addictive game conquered the world and launched a revolution in entertainment.

The mechanical clock, invented by European monks in the Middle Ages, regulated monastic life by ringing bells at regular intervals. It has since become an essential part of our daily lives.

The first sunglasses were worn by judges in China to hide their facial expressions. Made of smoked quartz, they were more a tool of concealment than protection against the sun's rays.

Great Writers and Their Works

J.K. Rowling, the British author, braved adversity and saw her work "Harry Potter" become one of the best-selling book series in the world. Her difficult beginnings only underscored the power of her vision.

Mark Twain, or Samuel Clemens, drew from the treasure of his childhood experiences to create universal tales such as "The Adventures of Tom Sawyer" and "The Adventures of Huckleberry Finn." These works have become symbols of rural America.

Victor Hugo, the French pen who breathed life into "Les Misérables," painted a dark but realistic picture of post-revolutionary France. His works continue to resonate in the hearts of audiences, centuries later.

Jane Austen is an unforgettable voice who captured the essence of English aristocratic society with novels such as "Pride and Prejudice" and "Emma." Her strong and independent female characters defied the stereotypes of her time.

F. Scott Fitzgerald immortalized the golden age of the 1920s in "The Great Gatsby," a nuanced exploration of the American dream and its flaws.

Gabriel García Márquez took his readers to worlds where the real and the fantastic coexist, thanks to his unique style of magical realism in novels like "One Hundred Years of Solitude."

George Orwell, with his dystopian novels like "1984" and "Animal Farm," offered biting critiques of society and totalitarian regimes, which remain relevant today.

Haruki Murakami has captivated the world with his intriguing fusions of reality and fantasy, as in "Kafka on the Shore" and "1Q84." His works are a journey into the irrational.

Agatha Christie, the "queen of mystery," challenged the minds of millions of readers with her complex plots and iconic detectives like Hercule Poirot and Miss Marple.

William Shakespeare, the great English playwright, gave the world stories of love, tragedy, and comedy that transcend time and culture.

Charles Dickens captured the essence of the Victorian era and its many social problems with works like "Oliver Twist" and "A Christmas Carol."

Jules Verne, the French visionary, fascinated the world with his adventure and science fiction stories, dreaming up generations of future explorers and scientists.

Mary Shelley, at the tender age of 19, created "Frankenstein," one of the first science fiction novels, a reflection on creation and morality.

Ernest Hemingway, with his clean and direct style, left an indelible mark on American literature through works like "The Old Man and the Sea."

Louisa May Alcott captured the joys and sorrows of family life in "Little Women," a work that continues to touch readers of all generations.

Leo Tolstoy delved into the complexity of human nature and society with epic novels like "War and Peace" and "Anna Karenina."

Oscar Wilde charmed and scandalized his society with his sharp wit and provocative works like "The Picture of Dorian Gray."

Emily Dickinson, the reclusive poet, left a poetic legacy of extraordinary depth and sensitivity, most of her works being discovered only after her death.

Roald Dahl delighted children and adults with fantastic and humorous stories like "Charlie and the Chocolate Factory."

Antoine de Saint-Exupéry, with "The Little Prince," managed to create a work that speaks to both children and adults, a philosophical fable that explores the nuances of humanity.

Each writer is a universe unto themselves, having contributed to shaping our understanding of the world, awakening our imagination, and challenging our thinking. Their works cross time and space, touching generations of readers long after their era.

Renewable Energies

Imagine a world where the sun's energy could power the entire planet for a year, and all that in just one hour of sunlight! Yes, you heard that right, just one hour! The sun, this celestial furnace, has such colossal potential that it's like a shining treasure in the sky, waiting to be tapped into its full potential.

Wind turbines, these modern giants that dance to the rhythm of the wind, are so imposing that some have blades longer than a football field. They rise majestically in our fields and along our coasts, their gigantic blades turning like wheels of fortune, generating clean and uninterrupted energy.

Think of hydroelectric dams, these engineering wonders that channel the raw power of water. The Three Gorges Dam in China, a colossus among them, is so powerful it can even influence the rotation of our planet, as if the Earth itself were a gigantic hamster in a wheel.

Algae, these often scorned aquatic plants, are actually the future superstars of fuel. They grow at a staggering rate and can be transformed into biofuel, opening up the possibility that these simple organisms could one day power our cars.

Geothermal energy, this hidden heat at the heart of our Earth, is like a dormant energy just waiting to be awakened. In Iceland, this heat is even used to warm houses, turning each home into a cocoon of warmth, as if the Earth were giving us a big warm hug.

The water from your shower should not be underestimated as it could have a second life as energy. Some cities are so futuristic they turn wastewater into energy, proving that recycling can go far beyond what we imagine, transforming it into a resource rather than waste.

Tides, this incessant ballet between the Earth and the Moon, have more to offer than mere waves. Their energy could be harnessed to power entire cities, making every rising and falling tide an opportunity to generate electricity.

The first solar power plant, a visionary project of the 19th century in New York, used mirrors to concentrate sunlight, a bit like a giant magnifying glass. This shows that the idea of using the sun as an energy source is far from new; it was just waiting for technology to catch up.

And what about eco-friendly cars? They represent the future of transportation, running on resources like hydrogen and compressed air. They prove that sustainable mobility is not a pipe dream, but a reality within reach.

All of this sounds fantastic, doesn't it? But it's important to remember that renewable energies are still like the little thumb of global energy production. However, they are growing rapidly, and who knows, they could well become the energy giant of tomorrow.

The Great Civilizations

Brace yourselves for a stunning journey through time and space, for history is full of surprises! Picture a time when the Mayas, long before telescopes, were already exceptional astronomers. Their calendar, based on stars and planets, was breathtakingly accurate.

Now, take a leap back and land in Carthage, that ancient city-state where nobles performed unimaginable sacrifices. Yes, they sometimes offered their own children to the gods during mysterious rituals. Chilling, isn't it?

And the Great Wall of China? Forget the idea that it's visible from space; that's a myth! In reality, it's a series of walls and fortifications, like a gigantic puzzle snaking across mountains and deserts.

Let's talk cleanliness. You'd never believe that the Indus Valley civilization had bathrooms and sewage systems over 4000 years ago! It's as if the ancient Indus were the inventors of modern comfort.

The Spartans, those formidable warriors, took their training seriously. Barely at the age of 7, they entered a merciless military academy. No time for child's play here!

Ever tried to remember your grocery list? The Incas didn't have paper or pens, but they used "quipus," knotted cords that served as external memory.

Next, head to Rome and its colossal Colosseum. Imagine a stadium filled with 50,000 people shouting and cheering for gladiators, exotic animals, and even reenacted naval battles!

The Mesopotamians were pioneers of writing. They etched cuneiform signs on clay tablets, creating the first "books."

The Egyptians, meanwhile, were obsessed with the afterlife. They embalmed their dead and placed them in treasure-filled tombs. You could say they took their farewells very seriously!

The Aztecs had a rather pessimistic view of the world's creation. According to them, the gods had already created and destroyed the world four times. It's like a cosmic reboot!

And what about the Library of Alexandria, that lost treasure of knowledge? It was so vast that its destruction is considered one of the greatest intellectual tragedies in history.

The Persians, organized as they were, already had a postal system! Roads and relay stations sped up mail delivery, much like the precursors to our modern postal system.

The Khmers, those extraordinary architects, designed colossal irrigation networks to feed their people. And of course, they also built Angkor Wat, that architectural masterpiece.

The Sumerian civilization was ahead of its time, with advanced knowledge in mathematics and astronomy. It's as if they had their own team of scientists and engineers.

The Maoris of New Zealand were incredible carvers. Their "Marae" or meeting places, were adorned with incredibly detailed wooden figures.

The Nabateans, those desert geniuses, knew how to survive in extreme conditions. They developed techniques to collect and store water at Petra, their rock-carved city.

The Vikings weren't just simple warriors; they were also navigators, traders, and explorers. Who knows, they might have been excellent candidates for a survival reality show!

The Olmecs, often considered the forerunners of the great Mesoamerican civilizations, are famous for their giant stone heads. It's still a wonder how they managed to sculpt them with such primitive tools.

The script of the Indus Valley civilization remains a mystery that even the best cryptographers have yet to solve. It's like a puzzle still waiting to be put together.

Finally, the ancient Greeks believed that their pantheon of gods lived on Mount Olympus. From there, these deities watched over and governed the world of humans, much like very, very powerful parents.

So, what a journey, right? History is an endless adventure, and it shows us that human imagination knows no bounds. So, when's your next exploration?

Haunted Places and Urban Legends

Hold tight, dear young explorers, for I am about to take you on an adventure through the most mysterious and haunted places on our planet! We start in Romania, at Bran Castle, often associated with Dracula, the most famous vampire in literature. But be warned, the true story of this castle with the vampire count is murkier than you might think!

Now, off to California, to the Winchester mansion, a house that even ghosts would call "home". Sarah Winchester, the owner, kept expanding it because she believed the house was haunted by the spirits of people killed by Winchester weapons.

Next stop, London, where the city's tower is so haunted it could be the headquarters of Britain's ghosts! Imagine bumping into Anne Boleyn, the beheaded former queen, wandering the corridors.

Think the White House is just a political place? Think again! It is said that Abraham Lincoln makes appearances from time to time. Perhaps he's still checking on political decisions?

Eastern State Penitentiary in Pennsylvania is now closed, but it seems some of its former residents are still there. Strange noises and apparitions have been reported. Could there be a ghost meeting there?

Ah, the White Lady! This legend is so popular that it is found in many countries. A mourning or betrayed woman who appears near lakes or roads, a true classic of horror stories!

In Paris, the Garnier Opera is not just a place for magnificent performances. It also has its own spectral tenant, a masked man who inspired the famous "Phantom of the Opera".

The Capuchin Catacombs in Palermo, Italy, are a museum of the afterlife. The mummified bodies are so well preserved that little Rosalia Lombardo seems to be simply sleeping.

Have you ever heard of the Loch Ness Monster in Scotland? Despite all the research, "Nessie" remains elusive. Who knows, maybe it's just a shy big eel?

Chillingham Castle in England is so haunted it could be the perfect setting for a horror film. Apparitions, screams, and the sounds of chains are on the menu. Ready for a night tour?

Clinton Road in New Jersey is not your usual road. Between phantom trucks, child ghosts, and strange rituals, it's a road you wouldn't want to take alone at night!

The Queen Mary, a liner moored in California, is like a hotel for ghosts. Between apparitions and unexplained noises, it's a stay you won't soon forget.

In Lyon, the Croix-Rousse station is the scene of apparitions of a young woman near the tracks. Perhaps she's still waiting for her train?

Waverly Hills Hospital in the United States is so haunted that even the doors close by themselves. Add to that the apparitions of deceased patients, and you have the recipe for a sleepless night.

In Scotland, the Overtoun Bridge is a real mystery. An inexplicable number of dogs are said to have jumped off. Researchers are still perplexed.

The Hoosac Tunnel in Massachusetts is like a reality show for ghosts. Between apparitions and strange voices, it's a place you'd rather avoid.

La Llorona, this Latin American legend, tells the story of a weeping mother searching for her drowned children. A truly frightening tale!

Edinburgh Fortress in Scotland is a place laden with history and specters. With all the battles and betrayals that have taken place there, it's not surprising that it's one of the most haunted places in the UK.

Finally, the Belchen road in Germany is a real catalogue of paranormal phenomena. Ghosts, apparitions, and even cars that behave strangely!

So, are you ready for your own paranormal adventure? Don't forget your flashlight, because in these places, even the ghosts might be afraid!

Traditional Games and Board Games

First stop: ancient India, where chess originated. It's not just a simple board game, but rather a simulation of epic battles between two armies! Each piece has its own role, just like in a real battle. Incredible, isn't it?

Now let's take a flight to China to discover the game of Go. With its gridded board and black and white stones, this game may seem simple. But don't be fooled! Its strategic depth is so vast that it would take a lifetime to master.

From China, we jump forward in time to the Roman Empire. Who would have thought that hopscotch, the game you draw with chalk on the sidewalk, was played by Roman children?

Heading to the United States during the Great Depression. Monopoly wasn't always the wild capitalism game you know. Originally, it was designed to teach the principles of economy and property. Quite ironic, isn't it?

Now let's go to France to play "Petits chevaux". This game will take you on a crazy race around a board. And luck plays a big role, so don't get mad if you lose!

Do you like board games with squares and pawns? Then checkers is for you! Although it looks like chess, its rules are completely different and there are many variants around the world.

Back to India for a royal game: Pachisi. This ancient game was so prized by kings that they played it on large boards on the ground, with servants as pawns!

Jacks, often made of bones or stones, are a skill game found in many cultures. It's a fun way to test your dexterity.

"Connect Four" is a fierce battle where each player tries to line up four of their tokens first. A pure strategy game!

"Happy Families" is another French gem. Who doesn't like to gather families like the "Boulanger" or "Roi" family?

Next, we have "Shogi", the Japanese chess. This game has an amazing particularity: you can use the pieces you capture against your opponent!

"Battleship" is your chance to become a real admiral. Dive into a strategic aquatic duel where you try to sink your opponent's fleet.

"Mahjong" is much more than a computer solitaire game. In reality, it's an exciting group game that comes from China.

"Belote", very popular in France, is a card game for four players that requires good cooperation with your partner. Are you ready to team up?

"Backgammon" is one of the oldest games in the world, dating back 5000 years in Mesopotamia. Talk about a game that has stood the test of time!

"Uno" is a modern game where you must get rid of all your cards by following the color or number of the previous card. Simple but addictive!

"Dominoes" is another ancient game, coming from China in the 13th century. It's a chain reaction in power!

"Jenga" tests your nerves and dexterity. Remove the wooden blocks without toppling the tower, and you'll be the champion!

"Carcassonne" allows you to build your own medieval landscape with tiles. Each game is a new adventure!

Finally, "Tarot" is more than just a card game. In France, it is very popular and is played with a special set of cards. But beware, it is also used for divination!

The Heroes of the Resistance

Jean Moulin. This courageous man unified the disparate movements of the Resistance under a single banner, becoming a thorn in the side of the Gestapo. Tragically, he was betrayed and captured, but his legacy remains indelible.

Moving on to an extraordinary woman: Simone Veil. A Holocaust survivor, she transformed her pain into strength, becoming a tireless advocate for women's rights in France. She played a key role in legalizing abortion, thus changing the lives of millions of women.

The Manouchian group, a diverse ensemble mainly composed of immigrants, displayed incredible courage by sabotaging Nazi operations in Paris. Their diversity was their strength, their unity their shield.

Lucie Aubrac, a teacher by profession, proved that love can triumph over hate. With meticulous planning, she orchestrated the escape of her husband Raymond from the clutches of the Gestapo in 1943. A true epic of love and resistance.

Joachim Roncin crystallized the spirit of modern resistance with his slogan "Je suis Charlie" after the attack on Charlie Hebdo in 2015. This simple slogan became a rallying cry against intolerance and for freedom of expression.

The Shelburn network is another fascinating chapter in this story. This group helped over 130 Allied airmen escape Nazi occupation. A daring operation that saved many lives.

Andrée Borrel, a fearless parachutist, was one of the first women to be sent into occupied France. Captured and executed by the Nazis, she nonetheless left an indelible mark in the history of the Resistance.

Germaine Tillion, an ethnologist, used her expertise to document the atrocities committed by the Nazis. She survived the horror of the concentration camps and became a major voice for human rights.

Colonel Fabien, whose real name was Pierre Georges, marked the beginning of armed actions of the Resistance by executing a German officer in the Paris metro. An act that inspired many resistance fighters.

In the village of Le Chambon-sur-Lignon, Pastor André Trocmé and his community saved thousands of Jews from deportation. A heroic act of compassion and collective resistance.

Let's not forget Nancy Wake, a spy and resistance fighter of New Zealand origin who was one of the most decorated women of World War II. She became a legend in France under the name of "The White Mouse".

Rose Valland is another incredible woman who played a key role during the war. An art historian, she secretly worked to document artworks stolen by the Nazis. Thanks to her courage, countless treasures were returned to their rightful owners.

Discover the group of 23 from Grenoble, a band of students who, armed with simple leaflets and their courage, decided to resist Nazi propaganda. Although they were arrested and executed, their message of resistance was heard by thousands.

Then there's Joséphine Baker, an American artist who adopted France as her homeland. During the war, she used her career as a cover to spy on the Nazis, demonstrating that resistance can take many forms.

Louis Aragon, the writer and poet, also played a role in the Resistance. His works served as a source of inspiration and morale for those fighting against the occupation. His poem "Strophes pour se souvenir", in particular, became an anthem for the Manouchian group.

Pénélope Aubin, journalist and writer, was also a major player in the Resistance. Using her pen as a weapon, she wrote clandestine articles that galvanized the French population against the occupation.

Franceska Mann, a Polish dancer, showed incredible bravery when she attacked an SS guard in Auschwitz camp, demonstrating that even under the most terrible conditions, the human spirit can rise against oppression.

Jean-Pierre Levy, a leader of the French Resistance, founded the "Franc-Tireur" movement which was one of the first to organize into a network. His actions inspired other groups to follow his example, thus unifying the resistance against the enemy.

Discover the story of Mathilde Carre, a controversial figure who initially worked for the Resistance before becoming a double agent for the Nazis. Her story shows the complexity and moral dilemmas many people faced during the war.

And finally, let us honor the memory of Boris Vildé, an ethnographer and resistor who was among the first to be executed for his actions against the Nazi regime. Although he paid the ultimate price, his courage and sacrifice continue to inspire new generations.

And finally, let's honor the memory of Boris Vildé, an ethnographer and resistance fighter who was among the first to be executed for his actions against the Nazi regime. Although he paid the ultimate price, his courage and sacrifice continue to inspire new generations.

Weather Phenomena

First stop: the equatorial Pacific Ocean, where we will meet El Niño. This capricious character warms the ocean waters and creates climatic chaos worldwide, from droughts in Australia to floods in South America. But beware, its twin sister, La Niña, is no less intriguing. She does the exact opposite, cooling the waters and disrupting the climate in her own way.

Next, we head to the polar regions to witness a breathtaking light show: the auroras borealis. These dancing lights are created by the interaction between solar particles and the Earth's atmosphere. A true cosmic ballet!

Then, on to the United States' Tornado Alley, where tornadoes, these rotating columns of air, are part of the landscape. These wind giants are classified on the Fujita scale, which measures their destructive power. Hold on tight, it's going to be a bumpy ride!

To change the atmosphere, let's head to Southeast Asia to experience the monsoon. This phenomenon is like a massive breath that brings torrential rains, transforming arid landscapes into lakes and rivers.

Speaking of water, do you know what a tropical cyclone is? Called hurricanes or typhoons depending on their location, these swirling monsters can devastate anything in their path. Their strength is measured in km/h, and they are far from being winds to take lightly.

Ah, heatwaves! Who would have thought that simple high temperatures could cause so much havoc, from droughts to wildfires?

But beware, the climate also has its little secrets, like microbursts. These descending air currents can cause as much damage as tornadoes, but over a wider area. A real punch from nature!

And what about acid rain, blizzards, tsunamis, and even fish rains? Yes, you heard right, fish falling from the sky! The weather has more than one trick up its sleeve.

Ah, the sea mist, this mysterious veil that envelops the coasts like in a Sir Arthur Conan Doyle novel! Did you know it is made up of tiny droplets of seawater? A salty fog that adds a touch of mystery to our maritime explorations.

Sinkholes, these geological formations that seem to swallow the earth, are like doors to another world. Some are so deep they could engulf entire buildings. A natural abyss that sends shivers down your spine, doesn't it?

Let's talk about Lake Baikal in Siberia, the deepest and oldest lake in the world. It holds about 20% of the Earth's unfrozen freshwater. It's as if the planet is keeping its most precious treasure well hidden in this remote corner.

Imagine the power of fire and ice combined. In Iceland, volcanoes and glaciers coexist, creating a landscape worthy of a science fiction film. The earth rumbles and the ice melts, in an eternal dance between two opposing elements.

Ah, quicksand! This natural trap that has terrorized so many adventure film heroes is actually a mixture of sand, water, clay, and organic matter. A dangerous cocktail that can swallow objects in the blink of an eye!

The solar wind, this rain of charged particles ejected by the Sun, is capable of disrupting our communication systems. Imagine billions of tiny archers, shooting their invisible arrows through space.

Geysers, these hot water jets that spring from the earth, are geothermal wonders. The Great Geyser in Iceland can shoot water up to 70 meters high! It's as if the Earth itself were blowing giant bubbles.

Let's move on to a meteorological mystery: fireballs, or ball lightning. This rare phenomenon appears during storms and moves defying the laws of gravity. A true electrical UFO!

And what do you think of mammatus clouds, these clusters of clouds that look like pouches hanging in the sky? They are often the harbinger of violent storms. It's as if the sky itself were sending us a warning.

Red rains, these tinted precipitations that seem out of a horror movie, are actually caused by microorganisms or suspended particles. A rain that, instead of washing, stains everything in its path.

Exotic Fruits and Vegetables

Our first stop takes us to Central America to discover the dragon fruit. Picture a vibrant pink fruit with green scales, containing a sweet, white flesh speckled with black seeds. Its antioxidants are like tiny soldiers ready to battle the free radicals in your body.

Next, we head to Southeast Asia to meet the king and queen of fruits: the durian and the mangosteen. The durian emits such a potent smell that it's banned in some public places, but its creamy flesh is a true delight for those daring enough to taste it. The mangosteen, with its purple robe and white flesh, is the perfect antithesis of the durian.

But wait, there's more! Have you ever seen a hairy lychee? The rambutan is exactly that, and its juicy flesh is a burst of vitamin C in your mouth.

In South America, we find the tamarillo, an exotic tomato that can be red, orange, or yellow. Its flesh is a sublime blend of sweetness and acidity.

Let's take a moment to salute the salak from Indonesia, nicknamed the "snake fruit" for its scaly skin. Its taste? A mix between apple, pineapple, and citrus.

But if you think these fruits are strange, wait until you meet the jackfruit, the largest fruit in the world, weighing up to 40 kg! Its sweet yellow flesh is so versatile that it can be used in both sweet and savory dishes.

And what about the starfruit, this star-shaped fruit that shines brightly on your plate, rich in vitamins and minerals?

We can't end this journey without mentioning the jicama from Mexico, often eaten raw with a bit of chili and lemon, and the goji berry from China, a superfood rich in antioxidants.

The Great Artists and Their Masterpieces

Let's begin with Claude Monet, the pioneer of Impressionism. Did you know that this great artist had failing eyesight? Indeed, some experts believe that his cataracts influenced his unique style, giving his famous water lilies that blurry and unreal quality.

Then, there's Georges Seurat, the inventor of pointillism. Imagine placing thousands of tiny dots of color on a canvas, creating an image that only emerges as you step back. His work "A Sunday Afternoon on the Island of La Grande Jatte" is a perfect example of this technique.

Ah, Salvador Dalí! Who can forget his melting clocks in the painting "The Persistence of Memory"? It's an invitation to ponder the nature of time itself.

And from Japan, we have Katsushika Hokusai. His "The Great Wave off Kanagawa" is such a powerful image that it has inspired artists and designers around the world.

Georgia O'Keeffe, the "Mother of American modernism," is best known for her oversized flowers and New Mexico landscapes. Her works make you see the world in a way you never considered.

M.C. Escher, on the other hand, plays with your mind. His drawings, like "Relativity," feature people defying the laws of gravity, walking in every possible direction.

René Magritte, with his work "The Treachery of Images" (commonly known as "This is Not a Pipe"), reminds us that art is not always what it seems to be. It's a profound reflection on reality and perception.

As for Andy Warhol, he managed to turn popular images, like that of Marilyn Monroe, into art. His "Marilyn Diptych" is a pop culture icon.

Edvard Munch and his painting "The Scream" perfectly capture human anguish. It's a work that draws you in and haunts you long after you've seen it.

Yayoi Kusama, the Japanese artist, invites you into a world full of dots. Her immersive installations are an experience in themselves, enveloping you in a universe of patterns and colors.

Ah, Banksy, the anonymous street artist whose works are as provocative as they are ephemeral. His drawings in the streets around the world make us reflect on our society.

And we can't forget Artemisia Gentileschi, one of the few female artists of her time, whose painting "Judith Beheading Holofernes" is a powerful symbol of female strength.

Finally, Marc Chagall takes us into a world where dream and reality merge, his works being a vibrant mix of his childhood in Belarus and his boundless imagination.

Ah, Vincent van Gogh, the tormented artist who created some of the most iconic works in the history of art. "The Starry Night" is like an open window into his soul, with its swirls of light and color.

Pablo Picasso, the master of Cubism, showed us that reality can be broken down into shapes and angles. His work "Guernica" is a heart-wrenching cry against the brutality of war.

Frida Kahlo, the Mexican artist, is an icon of feminism and resilience. Each of her self-portraits is an intimate page from her life journal, filled with pain and passion.

Jackson Pollock, the inventor of "dripping," a technique that involves dropping paint onto the canvas. His works are like maps of his subconscious, chaotic but fascinating.

Pieter Bruegel the Elder, who gives us a glimpse into the daily life of the medieval era. His "Peasant Wedding" is a true genre scene, where each character has their own story to tell.

Caravaggio, the master of chiaroscuro, whose paintings seem to emerge from the shadows to grip us with emotion. His "Judith Beheading Holofernes" is a scene as violent as it is beautiful.

Keith Haring, with his street art and pop icons, brought art to the masses. His simplistic but expressive drawings are an ode to diversity and inclusion.

Jean-Michel Basquiat, whose works are an explosive mix of text, symbols, and colors. His raw style and social engagement have left an indelible mark on the contemporary art world.

Leonardo da Vinci, not just an artist but also an inventor, a scientist, and a thinker. "Mona Lisa" with her mysterious smile continues to captivate the millions of visitors who flock to the Louvre each year.

Henri Rousseau, a customs officer by profession but an artist at heart. His painting "The Dream" is a lush jungle filled with mystery and exoticism, a true escape into another world.

The Life of the Samurai

Imagine yourself wearing armor designed to resemble a butterfly, believing that this appearance might distract or even intimidate your enemies. Quite clever, isn't it?

Even their smile was a status symbol, with teeth lacquered black, a fashion that might seem strange to us today but was a sign of beauty and sophistication at the time.

Their swords, the katanas, were considered living souls, forged with precision and extreme attention. It wasn't just a weapon; it was an extension of themselves.

But don't think that the samurai were merely warriors. They were often educated in the arts, like poetry and calligraphy, reflecting a depth and sensitivity that one might not suspect at first glance.

And yes, there were female samurai, known as onna-bugeisha. These formidable women took up arms and defended their homes in the absence of their husbands, proving that courage and honor were not reserved for men alone.

Wondering why their hairstyles were so elaborate? It was so their helmet would fit perfectly during battles. Every detail mattered, even the hair.

Tea also held great importance. The tea ceremony was an art form and meditation, a moment of calm and reflection amid the chaos of warrior life.

As for the frightening masks they wore, the mempo, they were designed to terrorize the enemy while providing essential protection against projectiles.

In times of peace, these warriors turned into farmers, never losing their status and privileges. It was a life of balance, between the art of war and the art of peace.

The Bushido code, "The Way of the Warrior," guided every aspect of their lives, emphasizing values like honor, loyalty, and courage. It was the moral pillar that upheld their existence.

And what about engaging in a poetic duel before an actual sword duel? It was a refined way to express mutual respect and the level of education between two adversaries.

Have you heard of ninjas, those spies and assassins of feudal Japan? Many people think they were like samurai, but no! Ninjas had their own set of skills, and they were often seen as the adversaries of samurai, acting in the shadows.

Samurai were also followers of Zen, a form of Buddhism that helped them stay focused and calm, even in the heart of battle. Imagine meditating peacefully while knowing you could be called to fight at any moment!

Do you like animals? Samurai did too! They often had hawks or eagles as companions for hunting. These birds of prey weren't just useful for catching game but were also status symbols.

Their armor was often adorned with symbols and mon, family emblems, which were like their own trademark. You could tell which family a samurai belonged to just by looking at the details of his armor.

Samurai used a unique form of archery, called kyūdō, or "the way of the bow." They even shot their arrows while on horseback, which required incredible skill and precision.

The philosophy of "Iaido" is equally fascinating. It's the art of quickly drawing the sword to slice one's enemy in a single motion, then sheathing the sword with the same fluidity. An art in itself!

Some samurai were also followers of "noh," a type of Japanese theater. They didn't just watch the plays but were also actors and patrons of this artistic genre.

Samurai had a very specific diet to stay in shape. They mainly ate rice, vegetables, and fish, avoiding meat for religious and ethical reasons.

Have you seen those banners that samurai wear on their backs, called "sashimono"? They served to identify soldiers on the battlefield, much like flags in modern armies.

Historical Monuments

The Eiffel Tower was built by Gustave Eiffel and his team for the 1889 Paris World's Fair, commemorating the centenary of the French Revolution. Standing at 324 meters tall, it was initially planned to be dismantled after 20 years, but its value as a telecommunications antenna ensured its survival.

The Great Wall of China stretches over more than 21,000 kilometers, though the preserved sections total about 6,000 kilometers. Begun in the 7th century B.C., its construction continued until the 17th century to protect China from invasions.

Stonehenge, located in Wiltshire, UK, was built between 3000 and 2000 B.C. Its massive stones, some weighing up to 25 tons, were transported over distances up to 240 kilometers, a remarkable logistical feat for the time.

The Parthenon, erected in 447 B.C. on the Acropolis of Athens, was dedicated to the goddess Athena. This masterpiece of Doric architecture was partially destroyed in 1687 when an ammunition depot inside exploded during the Venetian siege of Athens.

The Alhambra, located in Granada, Spain, is a complex of palaces and fortresses built mainly between 1238 and 1358. This monument is famous for its exquisite Islamic architectural details, inner courtyards, and fountains.

Mont Saint-Michel is an island commune in Normandy, France, famous for its Benedictine abbey. Known for being accessible on foot at low tide, it attracts over three million visitors each year.

Notre-Dame de Paris, completed in 1345 after nearly 200 years of construction, is an iconic example of Gothic architecture. It suffered a devastating fire in April 2019, which destroyed its spire and roof, but restoration efforts are underway.

La Sagrada Familia in Barcelona, Antoni Gaudí's unfinished masterpiece, has been under construction since 1882. It is funded exclusively by private donations and visitor entry fees, with a completion date planned for 2026, marking the centenary of Gaudí's death.

The Doge's Palace, located in Venice, was the residence of the Doges, the rulers of the Republic of Venice, and was built mainly in the 14th century. Its design blends Gothic and Byzantine influences, reflecting Venice's status as a major maritime power of the time.

The Sydney Opera House, designed by Danish architect Jørn Utzon and inaugurated in 1973, is one of the most distinctive and famous 20th-century buildings. Its cost was over 14 times the initial budget, but it is now recognized as a global architectural icon.

Neuschwanstein Castle in Bavaria, Germany, was built by King Ludwig II of Bavaria in 1869. Designed as a personal retreat rather than a fortress, it inspired Disneyland's Sleeping Beauty Castle.

Christ the Redeemer, a 30-meter-tall statue located atop Mount Corcovado in Rio de Janeiro, was completed in 1931. It is built of reinforced concrete and covered with thousands of soapstone triangles.

The Leaning Tower of Pisa, famous for its tilt, began to lean during its construction in the 12th century due to unstable soil. Its tilt was partially corrected in the 20th century, ensuring its stability for generations to come.

Charles Bridge in Prague was built in the 14th century under the reign of Emperor Charles IV. Featuring baroque statues and three guard towers, it is one of Europe's most famous bridges.

The Burj Khalifa in Dubai, completed in 2010, is the tallest building in the world at 828 meters. It required 22 million work hours and cost approximately 1.5 billion dollars to build.

The Acropolis in Athens, dating back to the 5th century B.C., houses structures such as the Parthenon and Erechtheion. It has served as a fortress, religious sanctuary, and is now one of the most visited archaeological sites in the world.

Angkor Wat in Cambodia, built in the 12th century by King Suryavarman II, is the largest religious complex in the world. Initially dedicated to the Hindu god Vishnu, it was converted into a Buddhist site in the 14th century.

Hagia Sophia in Istanbul was built in 537 under Byzantine Emperor Justinian I. It has served as a cathedral, mosque, and is now a museum, bearing witness to the region's rich religious and architectural history.

The Moscow Kremlin, a fortified complex at the heart of the city, was the residence of the tsars and is now the seat of the Russian government. Its walls were built in the 15th century, and the complex houses several cathedrals and palaces.

The Moai of Easter Island, built by the Rapa Nui people between 1250 and 1500, are monolithic statues weighing up to 82 tons. Their construction and transportation remain a mystery to researchers.

The Forbidden City in Beijing, constructed from 1406 to 1420, was the imperial palace of the Ming and Qing emperors. With over 980 buildings, it constitutes the largest preserved wooden structure complex in the world.

Wildlife

The African Elephant, for instance, is often dubbed the "forest gardener" because it helps to sow seeds over vast distances. Its memory is so remarkable that it can recall water points even during the most extreme drought seasons. Yet, this collective memory is threatened by poaching, targeting their valuable ivory tusks.

The Lion, this majestic carnivore, is known for its roar that can be heard up to 5 miles away. It's not just a hunting call but also a territorial declaration. The color and density of a male's mane can even reveal its health and age.

The Cheetah, the animal kingdom's Formula 1 racer, can reach speeds of up to 70 mph in just a few seconds. However, this born sprinter must rest after each exhausting race, leaving its prey vulnerable to thieves like hyenas or lions.

The Black Rhinoceros, despite its imposing size, has quite limited vision, not exceeding 30 meters. It compensates for this with a highly developed sense of smell and hearing. Its horn, made of keratin, is unfortunately highly prized on the black market.

The Giraffe, this living skyscraper, has a heart weighing up to 25 pounds to pump blood up to its brain, nearly 20 feet above. No small feat!

The Zebra, with its distinctive stripes, creates an optical illusion when in a group, making it difficult for predators to target an individual during a hunt. Each zebra has a unique set of stripes, like human fingerprints.

The Mountain Gorilla, this distant cousin, uses a series of grunts, howls, and even facial expressions to communicate within its group. It's incredibly social and lives in families led by a dominant silverback male.

The Hippopotamus, despite its chubby appearance and slow gait, can run up to 15 mph and is incredibly territorial. It kills more humans each year than any other large mammal in Africa.

The Nile Crocodile, this prehistoric predator, has a bite that can exert pressure of nearly 3700 pounds per square inch (psi), capable of crushing bones like glass.

The Meerkat, this small mammal, lives in colonies and uses a sophisticated surveillance system, where members take turns keeping watch. Their communication system is so complex it even includes specific "words" for different types of predators.

The Fennec Fox, this sand-dwelling fox, has oversized ears that serve not only to pick up sounds miles away but also to dissipate heat in the scorching desert. It's like a living radar, alert to the slightest danger.

The Tasmanian Devil, despite its frightening name, is a nocturnal marsupial that can emit terrifying howls to ward off predators. But in reality, it's a rather shy animal that prefers flight over fight.

The Okapi, this mysterious relative of the giraffe, hides in the dense forests of Central Africa. Its leg stripes often lead to confusion with the zebra, but it's an excellent means of camouflage in its forest environment.

The Narwhal, often dubbed the "unicorn of the sea," is famous for its long, spiraled tooth that can measure up to 10 feet. This "horn" is actually a highly sensitive tooth that helps it detect changes in its marine environment.

The Kakapo, this New Zealand parrot, is a critically endangered species. Despite its ability to mimic complex sounds, including mechanical noises, it's unfortunately incapable of flight.

The Manatee, this "sea cow," is a peaceful herbivore that spends most of its life grazing on aquatic plants. Contrary to what one might think, it's quite agile in water, thanks to its powerful caudal fin.

The Bullet Ant, living in tropical forests, has one of the most painful stings in the animal kingdom. The pain is so intense it's likened to that of a bullet, hence its name.

The Peacock Spider, small but colorful, is known for its spectacular mating dance where the male displays his vibrant colors to attract a mate. It's like a seduction dance in the wild.

The Panther Chameleon, native to Madagascar, can change the color of its skin to communicate its mood, regulate its temperature, or camouflage itself. It's a true chameleon in every sense of the word!

The Three-toed Sloth, this paragon of slowness, moves so slowly that algae grow on its fur, offering natural camouflage. But don't be fooled, its slowness is a survival strategy to go unnoticed by predators.

Balloon and Airship Journeys

The first hot air balloon flight by the Montgolfier brothers in 1783 was not just a technical feat, but also a pivotal moment in mankind's perception of its own limitations. This 10-minute flight, covering 2 km, forever changed our relationship with the sky.

The Zeppelin, an early 20th-century engineering masterpiece, embodied the promise and elegance of aviation. It was also a symbol of luxury, with lounges, restaurants, and even a music hall on board. However, the Hindenburg tragedy in 1937, where flammable hydrogen caused a fatal fire, marked a turning point, giving way to safer helium.

The crossing of the English Channel in 1785 by Jean-Pierre Blanchard and John Jeffries was a perilous adventure that captivated the world. They even had to throw out their ballast and clothes to succeed in the crossing!

Today, balloon technology has evolved considerably. Gondolas are now equipped with meteorological instruments, GPS, and sophisticated communication systems. Pilots use these tools to navigate, exploiting air currents at different altitudes to change direction.

Modern airships, with their cargo capacities and low environmental impact, are experiencing a renaissance. They are envisioned for various applications, from freight transport to ecological tourism. The airship might well become a means of transportation of the future again.

Balloon festivals have become true celestial celebrations, where balloons of all shapes and sizes dance in the sky. It's a breathtaking visual spectacle that attracts thousands of people.

The Great Scientists

Isaac Newton, the esteemed English physicist, formulated the fundamental laws of classical mechanics inspired by a simple observation: an apple falling from a tree. He also laid the groundwork for calculus, a branch of mathematics that has become essential in nearly all scientific fields.

Marie Curie, the trailblazing woman, revolutionized physics and chemistry with her discovery of radium and polonium. She paved the way for significant advances in medicine and energy, but at a high cost, succumbing to aplastic anemia induced by radiation exposure.

Albert Einstein, the German prodigy, gifted us the theory of relativity. He revolutionized our understanding of time, space, and matter, even predicting extraordinary cosmic phenomena like black holes.

Galileo, the father of modern astronomy, defied ecclesiastical censorship to validate Copernicus's heliocentric theory. His discovery of Jupiter's moons provided direct evidence that not everything revolves around the Earth, a fact that led to his condemnation by the Church.

Charles Darwin, the HMS Beagle adventurer, forever altered our understanding of life on Earth. His theory of evolution by natural selection was one of the most groundbreaking and controversial ideas in science.

James Clerk Maxwell, the Scottish physicist, unified the fields of electricity and magnetism into one theory. His equations underpin everything from modern communication technologies to energy systems.

Rosalind Franklin, often overlooked yet pivotal, captured the famous "Photo 51" that enabled the discovery of DNA's structure. She stands as a striking example of the lack of recognition that women in science have often endured.

Niels Bohr, the Danish genius, pioneered quantum mechanics. His atomic model explained why atoms don't implode and how they emit light.

Barbara McClintock, the daring geneticist, discovered "jumping genes," a finding that was ignored for decades before it was finally acknowledged and awarded a Nobel Prize.

Alan Turing, the English mathematician and logician, laid the foundations for modern computing and helped end World War II by decrypting the German Enigma machine. He also became a symbol for the gay rights movement after being persecuted for his sexual orientation.

Stephen Hawking, born in 1942 in England, became a legend in theoretical physics despite a diagnosis of amyotrophic lateral sclerosis (ALS) that gradually paralyzed him. He is best known for his work on black holes and cosmology, and his book "A Brief History of Time" made complex science accessible to the public.

Ada Lovelace, born in 1815 in England, is often regarded as the first computer programmer. The daughter of the poet Lord Byron, she collaborated with Charles Babbage on the "Analytical Engine," a mechanical device intended to carry out mathematical operations. Ada recognized the machine's potential far beyond arithmetic calculations and wrote the first algorithm intended to be processed by such a machine.

Rachel Carson, born in 1907 in the United States, was a marine biologist and conservationist whose book "Silent Spring" catalyzed the modern environmental movement. Her work led to public awareness of the dangers of chemical pesticides and ultimately to the establishment of the United States Environmental Protection Agency (EPA).

André-Marie Ampère, born in 1775 in France, laid the foundations of electromagnetism and electrodynamics. He was the first to demonstrate that two parallel wires carrying an electric current attract or repel each other, a discovery that led to the definition of the ampere, the unit of electric current.

Srinivasa Ramanujan, born in 1887 in India, was a self-taught mathematician who made enormous contributions to number theory, series, and functions. Despite never having formal training in mathematics, his genius was recognized by European mathematicians of his time, and he was elected a Fellow of the Royal Society of London.

Jane Goodall, born in 1934 in the UK, is a primatologist and anthropologist who transformed our understanding of chimpanzees. She was the first to observe that chimpanzees use tools, a trait previously thought to be exclusively human.

World Cuisines

Australian cuisine is an eclectic blend influenced by British and Mediterranean culinary traditions, as well as Asian cooking. The "barbie," or barbecue, is an institution, as is Vegemite, a yeast-based spread.

Argentinian cuisine is renowned for its high-quality beef, often grilled on a barbecue or "asado." Empanadas, stuffed pastries, are also a popular dish, as is dulce de leche, a milk-based jam.

Cuban cuisine is a mix of Spanish, African, and Caribbean flavors. "Ropa vieja," a dish of shredded beef stewed with vegetables, is considered a national dish. Cubans are also fond of malanga, a local tuber.

Polish cuisine is hearty and substantial, making extensive use of potatoes, cabbage, and meats. "Pierogi," a type of dumpling, and "kielbasa" sausage are emblematic dishes. "Barszcz," a beet soup, is often consumed during holidays.

Egyptian cuisine, one of the oldest in the Middle East, is simple yet flavorful. "Koshary," a dish of rice, lentils, and pasta, is considered the national dish. "Ful medames," a fava bean puree, is another staple.

Filipino cuisine is a fascinating blend of Malay, Chinese, Spanish, and American influences. "Adobo," a dish of marinated and stewed meat in soy sauce and vinegar, is popular. "Lumpias," spring rolls, are also highly appreciated.

Nepalese cuisine is heavily influenced by its Indian and Tibetan neighbors. "Dal bhat," a dish of lentils and rice, is a staple, often accompanied by curried vegetables and "achar" (condiments).

Emirati cuisine makes abundant use of lamb and chicken, often stewed with spices and served with rice. Seafood, including shrimp and fish, is also popular, as is "shawarma," a grilled meat sandwich.

Norwegian cuisine is heavily influenced by its coastal environment. "Klippfisk," dried cod, is a staple, as is "rakfisk," fermented fish. "Lefse," a type of flatbread made with potatoes, is often consumed during festivities.

Lebanese cuisine is a symphony of Mediterranean and Middle Eastern flavors. "Hummus," a chickpea puree, is a staple, as is "tabbouleh," a salad of fresh parsley. And let's not forget "baklava," a sweet pastry made with honey and nuts.

Thai cuisine is a delicate balance of sweet, salty, sour, and spicy. "Pad Thai," a stir-fried noodle dish, is known worldwide. Thai green curry, meanwhile, is an intoxicating blend of coconut milk, green chilies, and basil.

Mexican cuisine is an explosion of flavors and colors. "Tacos," filled tortillas, are as varied as they are delicious. And what about "guacamole," a spicy avocado puree that accompanies almost every dish?

Swedish cuisine is often associated with the "smörgåsbord," a buffet of various cold dishes. "Gravlax," marinated salmon, and "köttbullar," famous meatballs, are specialties that warm the heart.

Senegalese cuisine is rich in flavors and spices. "Thieboudienne," a dish of fish, rice, and vegetables, is often considered the national dish. "Yassa," a dish of chicken or fish marinated in a lemon-onion sauce, is also highly favored.

Greek cuisine is a tribute to olive oil, herbs, and fresh vegetables. Moussaka, an eggplant and minced meat casserole, is a comforting dish. "Souvlakis," meat skewers, are often eaten as a sandwich in pita bread.

Peruvian cuisine is a fusion of indigenous, European, and Asian traditions. "Ceviche," raw fish marinated in lemon juice, is an emblematic dish. "Lomo saltado," a beef stir-fry with vegetables, reflects Chinese influences.

South African cuisine is a mix of various cultures, from Malay influences to indigenous traditions. "Bobotie," a minced meat dish with an egg cream layer, is a fascinating example of this melting pot.

Russian cuisine is more than just "borscht," a beet soup. "Stroganov," beef in a creamy sauce, and "pelmenis," meat-stuffed dumplings, offer a glimpse into the country's culinary richness.

Lighthouses and Their Significance

The Ar-Men lighthouse in France is like the superhero of lighthouses. Constructing this tower amidst the tempestuous sea was such an epic quest that it took nearly 15 years to complete! Meanwhile, the Jeddah lighthouse in Saudi Arabia decided to grow tall, becoming the world's tallest lighthouse at a towering 133 meters — that's like stacking 26 giraffes on top of one another!

But wait, lighthouses aren't just there to look pretty or break records. Some serve as weather stations, others are like hotels where you can spend the night. It used to be the lighthouse keeper who took care of everything. Imagine living alone in a lighthouse, ensuring the light never goes out. Nowadays, thanks to technology, most of these lighthouses operate autonomously.

If we turn back the clock, the very first known lighthouse, the Lighthouse of Alexandria in Egypt, was so astounding that it was listed as one of the Seven Wonders of the Ancient World. And guess what? The lens system that makes lighthouse beams so powerful was invented by a Frenchman named Augustin-Jean Fresnel. It's as though someone figured out how to turn a simple flashlight into a super spotlight!

And speaking of spooky stuff, some lighthouses are said to be haunted. Tales suggest that the spirits of former keepers come back to check that all is well. Creepy, right? But on the flip side, these isolated towers are so picturesque that artists come from all over just to paint or photograph them.

In Ireland, there's a lighthouse called Fastnet Rock. It's known as "Europe's last lighthouse" because it's the last sight you see when leaving the continent for America. It's a bit like bidding farewell to an old friend.

Lighthouses have also been witnesses to great historical moments. They've served as beacons in naval battles and even aided distressed aircraft during wars. Despite advancements in technology, like GPS, lighthouses continue to play a crucial role, especially in places where modern gadgets might fail you.

Each lighthouse has a kind of "light signature," a unique pattern that helps mariners identify which one they're seeing. It's like a luminary ID card! And they're not only famous in the real world but also in movies and books where they often symbolize hope and constancy.

Lighthouses have their legends and myths as well. Take the Minou lighthouse in Brittany, which has a little cat statue at its base. Legend has it that this cat brings good luck to sailors passing near the lighthouse. It's like a talisman for protection at sea!

Some lighthouses have even played a role in heroic rescues. The Skerryvore lighthouse in Scotland, for example, helped guide a ship in distress during a ferocious storm, saving lives that would have been lost in the tumultuous waters.

Speaking of storms, you'd be amazed to learn that the Bell Rock lighthouse in Scotland is built on a rock that's submerged at high tide! Builders had to race against time at each low tide to construct it. Talk about a challenge!

And if you like mysteries, the Eilean Mor lighthouse in Scotland is shrouded in one. In 1900, the three lighthouse keepers vanished without a trace. The logbook described strange storms, but no other signs were found. The mystery remains unsolved to this day.

Lighthouses are not just made of stone or metal; some are made of wood, like the charming Pachena Bay lighthouse in Canada. It even has a quaint little house next to it for the keeper to live with their family. It's almost like a life-size dollhouse!

Let's not forget about modern lighthouses, like the Jeddah lighthouse, which is not only the tallest in the world but also made entirely of concrete. It's like a modern-day giant watching over the seas.

Some lighthouses have even found a second life. The Gatteville lighthouse in France has been transformed into a museum where you can learn more about the lives of lighthouse keepers and the maritime history of the region. A real gem for the curious!

Lighthouses have also become popular tourist destinations. The Byron Bay lighthouse in Australia offers breathtaking ocean views and is an excellent vantage point for whale watching during migration.

In Japan, the Osezaki lighthouse is considered a sacred place, and many visitors come to pray for safety at sea. It's a fascinating blend of technology and spirituality.

The Fascinating World of Insects

Ah, insects! These tiny creatures that we see everywhere, from gardens to forests, and even in our homes. You might not believe it, but there are more insects on Earth than there are stars in our galaxy! Yes, you heard that right. And that's not all: we haven't even discovered all the types of insects that exist yet. It's like a vast hidden treasure of biodiversity.

Let's talk about ants. These tiny workers are real living fossils! They were around long before the dinosaurs and have survived cataclysms that would make even the bravest superhero tremble.

Speaking of remarkable feats of nature, are you familiar with monarch butterflies? They travel distances equivalent to a human walking from Paris to Moscow. The craziest part is that they make this journey without GPS, without a map, and without having done it before.

But wait, there's something even more astonishing! The bombardier beetle has its own version of a super-powerful jet. No, it's not an airplane, but when it feels threatened, it can create a small chemical explosion to ward off the bad guys. It's like a miniature superhero!

Insects are not only survivors or adventurers; they are also true artists. Fireflies, for example, put on their own light show in the summer. Thanks to a chemical reaction in their bellies, they twinkle in the dark to woo their future mate. It's like a natural fireworks display!

And there's more! Some insects are also architects, doctors, and even musicians. Solitary bees make cozy homes for themselves without needing to share with a large family. Termites, often considered destroyers, are actually excellent gardeners who enrich the soil. And crickets, ah, they make music by rubbing their legs together. It's as if every insect has its own hidden talent.

Oh, and before I forget, some insects are even our allies. The honeybee, for example, gives us honey, this sweet delight that helps soothe sore throats. Cochineal insects, those little bugs, are fashion and beauty stars because they produce a red dye used in lipsticks and candies.

Insects are even present in the world of cinema and literature. Who can forget Kafka's "The Metamorphosis," which makes us reflect on identity and transformation, or the ants in the animated film "A Bug's Life," teaching us lessons about teamwork and perseverance?

There are also insects that are excellent at camouflage. The stick insect, for instance, looks so much like a twig that you might pick it up thinking it's real! It's like a little spy from nature.

And what about the cicada, this insect that sings all summer long? In La Fontaine's fable, it is seen as carefree, but did you know that some species of cicadas spend up to 17 years underground only to emerge and live for a few weeks? It's a life cycle that commands respect.

Ladybugs, those little spotted creatures we love so much, are real warriors in the garden. They hunt aphids and protect your plants.

Next time you see one, know that you have a tiny heroine by your side.

Insects even have their own version of society. Think of the leaf-cutter ants that grow their own food by cutting pieces of leaves to cultivate fungi. It's like a little underground farm!

Dragonflies, these insects with transparent wings, are among the oldest flying insects. They were already here long before birds took flight. Plus, they are excellent hunters, capable of capturing mosquitoes in mid-air.

The glow-worm, this little insect with luminous properties, isn't just a spectacle for the eyes. Its glowing abdomen is used to attract a mate but also to ward off predators by mimicking the appearance of other more dangerous insects.

History of the Olympic Games

Just imagine: more than 2500 years ago in ancient Greece, the first Olympic Games were held. Back then, there were no high-tech gyms or super sleek sports attire. Everything took place in Olympia, a sacred site dedicated to Zeus, the king of the gods. Picture men, and only men (yes, girls were left out!), running barefoot in a simple footrace. No gold, silver, or bronze medals, just an olive wreath for the champion. Pretty cool, right?

Then, one day, the Olympics disappeared. Why? Because the Roman Empire changed religions and decided these games were "pagan." It took almost 1500 years for a Frenchman named Pierre de Coubertin to say, "Well, if it was cool back then, why not revive it?" And so, in 1896, the modern Olympic Games were reborn in Athens!

The marathon, that super long 42-km sprint, was inspired by a Greek messenger who ran non-stop to announce a great victory. And those five rings you always see? They represent the five continents of the world, all united by the love of sport.

But the Olympics haven't always been smooth sailing. They've seen their share of dramatic moments, like when Jesse Owens snagged four gold medals in 1936 right under Adolf Hitler's nose! Or when Tommie Smith and John Carlos raised their fists in 1968 to fight against racism. Sadly, they've also seen tragedies, like the Munich hostage crisis in 1972.

Then there's the Olympic flame, that fire that travels from Olympia to the host city of the Games. It's like a baton passed between athletes, but here, it's entire countries passing it on, symbolizing unity and friendship.

If you're into more "trendy" sports, you'll be pleased to know the Games are evolving! Sports like skateboarding, surfing, and climbing have joined the party. And let's not forget the Paralympic Games, which remind us that sports are for everyone, regardless of your abilities.

The Olympics also reflect society and social changes. Consider the gradual introduction of women's events. Initially excluded, women now compete in almost all disciplines, with some like Simone Biles or Katie Ledecky even becoming legends.

But it's also a time when politics and sport intersect, sometimes controversially. During the Cold War, the Games were often a show of force between the United States and the Soviet Union. Who could forget the "Miracle on Ice" in 1980, when an inexperienced American team defeated the Soviets in ice hockey?

And let's not overlook the mascots, those often cute creatures designed for each Games. They bring a touch of fun and are adored by kids. From Waldi, the dachshund of Munich in 1972, to Miraitowa and Someity from Tokyo 2020, each mascot has its own story.

The Olympic oath, a promise made by one athlete on behalf of all, emphasizes the importance of fairness, honor, and respect. These are universal values that transcend borders and generations.

And for those who love numbers, the Olympics are a treasure trove of statistics. Sprinter Usain Bolt holds the world record for the 100 meters at 9.58 seconds. Michael Phelps, the human fish, has won a staggering 23 gold medals in swimming.

But beyond the medals and records, the Olympics are a celebration of human endeavor, determination, and excellence. Every athlete, win or lose, is a reminder of the incredible potential we all have within us.

Thus, the Olympics are not just a sporting event but a cultural and social phenomenon that captures the world's imagination. They show us the best and sometimes the worst of what we are, but above all, they unite us in a global celebration of humanity.

The Evolution of Cartoons

The first stop on our time travel is in 1928, right in the heart of New York. Imagine the wonder of seeing Mickey Mouse come to life for the first time in "Steamboat Willie". It wasn't just a first for Mickey, but for the entire animated film world. The audience was so enchanted that they gave a standing ovation!

Speaking of firsts, did you know that the very first "anime" originated in Japan in 1917? Yes, long before Pokémon took over our screens, there was "Namakura Gatana", a short samurai tale that lasted just four minutes. And it didn't even need subtitles!

Now let's move on to something a bit more recent but equally astonishing. In "Snow White and the Seven Dwarfs", it took more than two million sketches and 750 artists to create just 83 minutes of pure enchantment. Talk about a collective effort!

And speaking of Pokémon, did you know that the series was so popular that it even had to pull an episode due to health impacts? Yes, the flashing lights caused seizures in several viewers. Talk about an unexpected side effect of "Pokémania".

Remember "Toy Story"? This masterpiece was nearly erased forever, saved at the last minute by an employee who had a backup copy at home. Phew, what a relief, right?

Now let's head east and talk about Hayao Miyazaki. Believe it or not, this man draws all his films by hand! No computers, no shortcuts, just pure handcrafted art.

Have you seen "Kubo and the Two Strings"? Every second of this stop-motion film required hours and hours of painstaking work. A single 3.5-minute scene took one year to complete. Incredible, isn't it?

What about "The Simpsons"? This series, which started in 1989, has more seasons than some of you have years! It's the longest-running animated series in history, and it shows no signs of slowing down.

Switching gears, did you know that Shrek could have had a very different voice? Chris Farley was supposed to be the original voice, but after his tragic passing, Mike Myers took over the role. And he even added a Scottish twist to our favorite ogre!

Let's talk about "Avatar: The Last Airbender". This animated series was so well-received that it not only got a sequel but also a film adaptation. Although the movie wasn't as well-received, the series continues to hold a special place in our hearts.

The world of animation is a veritable hotbed of creativity and innovation. Each work is like a time capsule, reflecting the techniques, values, and imagination of an era. From Mickey Mouse to the sophisticated creations of Studio Ghibli, these films and series are more than just entertainment; they are pieces of culture that transcend boundaries.

Through the lens of animation, one can also see the evolution of technology. While early animations were meticulously crafted frame by frame, modern technologies have opened new pathways, especially with 3D animation. But even with all these advanced tools, nothing replaces the human touch, as Hayao Miyazaki's handiwork shows.

The world of animation is also a place where cultures meet and blend. Japanese anime has inspired generations of creators around the globe, just as Western productions have found a loyal audience in Asia. It's a true cultural exchange, made stroke by stroke, frame by frame.

And let's not forget the often profound messages these works convey. Whether it's the importance of friendship and adventure in "Pokémon" or questions of identity and destiny in "Avatar: The Last Airbender", these stories go well beyond mere entertainment. They make us think, challenge us, and sometimes, change us.

The history of video games

Our adventure begins in 1972 with "Pong," the video game that started it all. You'd be surprised to learn that it wasn't actually the first virtual tennis game; Ralph Baer had created one before that. Pong was a simplified version, but it marked the beginning of the Atari era.

Then, let's meet the most famous plumber of all time: Mario. Did you know he was originally a carpenter? Yes, before he got into unclogging pipes, Mario was quite handy with a hammer and nails.

Ah, "Tetris," that addictive game with falling blocks. Did you know that its name comes from the Greek word "tetra," meaning "four"? Indeed, each block is composed of four squares. It's a little nugget of information that makes the game even more interesting, doesn't it?

Imagine Lara Croft's footsteps in "Tomb Raider" are actually the sound of a microwave. Yes, sound designers had to be very creative!

And let's talk about "Final Fantasy." The name may seem grandiose, but it was born from the belief that this would be its creator's last game. Luckily for us, that wasn't the case.

Do you like board games? How about a 1,680-hour game of "Monopoly" in "Street Fighter: Monopoly"? That's a record that gives a new definition to the word "endurance."

Moving on to "Minecraft," the giant of video games. Can you believe it was developed in just six days? Astonishing, isn't it?

And what about the first video game ban in Norway? Yes, "Mortal Kombat" was too violent for the Norwegian government, leading to a temporary ban.

Do you remember catching bugs in jars when you were young? Satoshi Tajiri, the creator of Pokémon, did too, and it inspired him to create the Pokémon game.

And finally, the famous Pac-Man. This round, yellow character who keeps eating was inspired by... a pizza missing a slice. A rather delicious source of inspiration, right?

The first "Easter egg" in a video game was created by Warren Robinett in the game "Adventure" for the Atari 2600. He hid his name in a secret room of the game, a revolutionary act at a time when game developers were not credited for their work.

The "Konami Code," a specific sequence of buttons, has become legendary and has appeared in numerous games and even some websites and movies. It was created for the game "Contra" to help players gain extra lives.

The first competitive artificial intelligence in a game was introduced in "Pac-Man." The ghosts had different personalities and strategies, making the game more complex and interesting.

The term "boss level" first appeared in the game "Doom." It referred to a particularly difficult level at the end of a series of easier levels.

The first game console to use CD-ROMs was the Sony PlayStation. This marked a turning point in the way games were manufactured and stored, allowing for more complex graphics and sounds.

The game "World of Warcraft" holds the Guinness World Record for the most popular MMORPG, with millions of active subscribers at its peak.

The first use of the term "video game" occurred in a 1973 article in "Creative Computing" magazine, although the concept had been around for years.

The character Sonic was created by Sega as a response to Nintendo's Mario. He became so popular that he even had his own series of comics and cartoons.

The game "Angry Birds" has been downloaded more than 2 billion times since its launch, making it one of the most popular mobile games of all time.

In the game "The Legend of Zelda: Ocarina of Time," the music was designed to adapt in real-time to the player's actions, a first in the field of video games.

The Superheroes Through the Ages

Imagine, if you will, a time before superheroes had taken flight in the pages of comic books. Let's travel back to ancient Greece, where figures like Hercules with their superhuman strength were the true precursors to the superheroes we know and love today.

Ah, Superman! The hero who started the modern genre in 1938. But would you be surprised to know that his creators sold him for only $130? A paltry sum for a character who would become a global icon.

And what about Wonder Woman, the Amazonian warrior armed with her lasso of truth? Her creator, William Moulton Marston, was also the inventor of the lie detector. A coincidence? I think not.

Stan Lee, that name rings in the annals of comic book history as a true legend. From Spider-Man to Iron Man, he created a pantheon of characters that have withstood the test of time and even made appearances in their cinematic adaptations.

Batman, the masked vigilante haunting the streets of Gotham, didn't just appear out of thin air. He draws his inspiration from various sources, including the works of Leonardo da Vinci. Fascinating, isn't it?

Ah, Wolverine, that X-Man with adamantium claws. Though often associated with the United States, he is actually Canadian. His real name? Logan.

Before wielding his shield against modern-day supervillains, Captain America was a propaganda tool during World War II. He fought against the Axis powers in the colorful pages of the comics of the time.

And who could forget Black Panther, the first African-origin superhero in American comics? Not just a hero but also a king, he paved the way for more diverse representation in comics.

But even superheroes have seen dark days. In the 1950s, they nearly vanished, relegated to the sidelines of popular culture. Fortunately for us, the 1960s brought a renaissance, with new faces and new teams.

And in the 80s and 90s, things took a darker and more complex turn. Works like "The Dark Knight Returns" showed that superheroes could be deeply flawed, challenging traditional notions of good and evil.

And let's not forget those who defied conventions, like Deadpool, known for breaking the fourth wall and speaking directly to readers.

It's fascinating to see how superheroes have evolved through the ages, isn't it? But it's not just their history that's interesting; it's also their impact on our culture and society.

Let's not forget the role of superheroines like Jean Grey, Storm, and Black Widow, who have helped shape a new generation of strong, intelligent, and independent women. These characters have helped break some of the gender stereotypes that persisted in popular culture.

Let's also talk about fashion. Superhero costumes have influenced not only cosplay but also haute couture. Designers have drawn from the aesthetics of these characters to create outfits that merge art and function.

Superheroes have also found their place in education. Teachers use comics to teach everything from literature to philosophy to science. What better way to learn physics than discussing how Flash can run faster than light?

And what about the economic impact? The superhero industry is worth billions, thanks to movies, merchandise, and video games. They've become a veritable money-printing machine for the companies that own them.

The influence of superheroes also extends to social and humanitarian causes. Characters like Superman and Spider-Man have been used in campaigns for everything from road safety to preventing smoking among youth.

And in the real world, the aura of superheroes inspires acts of bravery. How many times have we heard stories of ordinary people performing extraordinary acts and then citing superheroes as their inspiration?

Superheroes have also made their way into the world of technology. Researchers and scientists are striving to create gadgets and equipment that resemble those we see in comics, from exoskeletons to night-vision contact lenses.

They have also been used in political campaigns, where candidates often compare themselves to heroic figures in an effort to garner support. Whether it's justice, bravery, or leadership, superheroes embody qualities that many aspire to have.

And finally, the psychological impact. Superheroes give us a sense of hope and wonder, reminding us that each of us has the power to make a difference in the world, no matter how small.

The Famous Boy Bands and Girl Groups

Let's start with BTS, these South Korean boys who have literally conquered the planet. Their fandom, known as "ARMY," is not just a group of fans, but a dedicated legion playing an invaluable role in their meteoric rise to international success.

From South Korea to BLACKPINK, this K-pop girl group is a force to be reckoned with. Their single "How You Like That" has broken records on YouTube, becoming an anthem for an entire generation.

Let's not forget One Direction, these five Brits turned four, who emerged from "The X Factor" to become a true global phenomenon.

Even though the group is on hiatus, each member has found their own path in successful solo careers.

Fifth Harmony, another product of "The X Factor," this time from the American version. The group experienced ups and downs, notably with the departure of Camila Cabello, before ultimately disbanding in 2018.

Little Mix, these talented women from the UK, not only won "The X Factor" but also continued to evolve, releasing hits and touring the world.

CNCO, this Latin boy band, brings a unique blend of pop and Latin influences, creating a sound that is instantly recognizable and irresistibly danceable.

And what about Red Velvet? This fascinating group is known for their musical duality, capable of making you dance one moment and plunging you into deep reflection the next.

In the world of K-pop, EXO is another dominant force, with a unique concept of sub-groups singing in Korean and Mandarin, thus reaching a broad audience in Asia.

TWICE, yet another titan of K-pop, has captured the public's imagination with their viral hit "TT," a song that has become a true phenomenon.

If we venture to America, we find the Jonas Brothers. After a split and a hiatus, they returned to the spotlight in 2019, proving that brothers can really overcome everything.

The Beatles are often considered the first "boy band," although they transcended that category. But did you know that their first single, "Love Me Do," only reached the 17th place on the British charts? A modest start for the most influential rock band of all time.

Moving on to Destiny's Child. This iconic trio, led by Beyoncé, debuted in the 90s. But did you know that the group changed its lineup several times before becoming the legendary trio we know?

The Backstreet Boys, these idols of the 90s, were not always five. In fact, they started out as a trio. It was only after meeting Kevin Richardson that Nick Carter, AJ McLean, and Howie Dorough completed the group with Brian Littrell.

The Spice Girls, these queens of "Girl Power," were formed by a newspaper ad. In response to this ad, over 400 girls auditioned to become the next big pop sensation.

Let's not forget NSYNC, which saw the rise of Justin Timberlake. Did you know that the group's name is an acronym made up of the last letters of the original members' first names? Justin, Chris, Joey, Jason, and JC.

And what about TLC, this female trio of the 90s? Their hit "Waterfalls" was one of the first to address social issues like HIV and drug use in a genre often focused on love and relationships.

And the Pussycat Dolls, before becoming pop stars, they were actually a burlesque dance troupe.

The Evolution of Popular Toys

Let's begin our journey through time in ancient Egypt, where dolls were more than mere playthings; they were a reflection of society and culture. Fast forward to 1959, and here's Barbie, the doll that revolutionized the toy world and paved the way for franchises like Bratz and Monster High.

The 1960s brought us LEGO bricks, those little plastic blocks that sparked waves of imagination and creativity in children and adults alike.

And who could forget the Tamagotchis of the '90s? These electronic pets were a major milestone in the merging of toys and technology.

Then there's Furby, the interactive plush toy capable of "learning" and communicating, which became a craze at the end of the '90s.

Silly Bandz bracelets and Beyblades took over playgrounds in the early 2000s, closely followed by the essential Funko Pop figures.

Hatchimals and LOL Surprise brought the magic of "unboxing" to the toy world, offering kids the joy of surprise and discovery. Board games, meanwhile, have stood the test of time, with classics like Monopoly being reinvented for new generations.

Education hasn't been left out, with a rise in popularity of educational toys like robotics kits and STEM kits, merging learning with play. Matchbox and Hot Wheels mini cars continue to roar in the hearts of children, while video games have redefined our very understanding of what it means to "play."

Beanie Babies plush toys, once simple playthings, are now collectibles worth thousands of euros. Polly Pocket dolls and their miniature worlds marked a generation, just as drones for kids and connected toys like programmable robots are doing today.

And for those who love the tactile side of play, playdough and slime kits offer a sensory experience, while 3D puzzles push problem-solving skills to a new level.

Ah, the Rubik's Cube! This colorful puzzle from the '80s is much more than a toy. Did you know there are international competitions where people solve this cube in seconds? Incredible!

And let's talk about spinning tops! They have been around since ancient times, but today, with brands like Beyblade, they've been catapulted into the future with combat arenas and technical features.

Who would have thought that stones could become a toy? Yet, Pet Rocks were a real phenomenon in the '70s. Companion rocks sold in a box, with straw as a bed. Simplicity at its best!

Remember Sea-Monkeys? These tiny aquatic creatures that "come to life" when you add water were actually dormant shrimp! A true pocket aquarium.

Ah, Pokémon cards! Originally created as a collectible card game, they have become a global fever. Some rare cards now sell for thousands of euros!

Video games are not to be left out. The Atari 2600, launched in 1977, opened the door to the home video game industry, laying the groundwork for consoles like the PlayStation and Xbox.

And what about the electronic dance mats that invaded arcades in the 2000s? Inspired by the video game "Dance Dance Revolution," they gave a new twist to the concept of active play.

Let's not forget the Transformers robots, toys that are both vehicles and characters. Their popularity was such that they spawned a complete franchise, including movies and TV series.

Reborn dolls are hyper-realistic dolls designed to look like real babies. They are so lifelike that some people use them for emotional therapies. A fascinating dimension of the toy world!

Literary Sagas

On a train from Manchester to London, J.K. Rowling conceives the idea of a bespectacled young wizard, Harry Potter. What begins as a fleeting thought transforms into a global phenomenon, encompassing seven masterful volumes and an expanded universe.

In a similar vein, Suzanne Collins merges the brutality of war and the artifice of reality TV to create "The Hunger Games," a dystopia that captivates millions of readers. Meanwhile, Stephenie Meyer translates an enigmatic dream into a vampiric saga, "Twilight," that fascinates and divides readers worldwide.

Rick Riordan, aiming to help his own son who struggled with dyslexia and ADHD, creates Percy Jackson, a hero who turns weaknesses into strengths. Veronica Roth, while still a student, imagines a world fractured by factions in "Divergent," while James

Dashner draws from the works he cherished as a child to create "The Maze Runner."

Young authors also make waves. Christopher Paolini writes "Eragon" at the tender age of 15, seeing his work rise to international bestseller status. Philip Pullman delves into the epic poem "Paradise Lost" to weave the complexity of "His Dark Materials."

The internet plays a role as well. Cassandra Clare moves from Harry Potter fan fiction to creating her own enchanting universe in "The Mortal Instruments." Jeff Kinney, whose "Diary of a Wimpy Kid" was initially meant to be a book for adults, finds unexpected success with young readers.

Inspirations are diverse. Ransom Riggs uses old photographs to create "Miss Peregrine's Home for Peculiar Children," Daniel Handler draws from his own sense of alienation to write "A Series of Unfortunate Events," and Eoin Colfer describes his work "Artemis Fowl" as "Die Hard with fairies."

A pseudonym can also be a tool. Erin Hunter is actually a collective of authors behind "Warriors," and Myra Eljundir adopts an Icelandic pseudonym to write the "Kaleb" series, inspired by her own life.

Ah, the power of dreams! J.R.R. Tolkien, a philology professor, created Middle-earth, a fantastical land populated by elves, hobbits, and dragons, while recovering from an illness in a hospital during World War I. Thus was born "The Lord of the Rings," an epic that continues to captivate the world.

Fancy mysteries? Arthur Conan Doyle, a trained physician, creates Sherlock Holmes, drawing inspiration from one of his own professors. The detective becomes so popular that Doyle feels compelled to "resurrect" him after trying to kill him off in one of his stories.

And what of "Charlie and the Chocolate Factory"? Roald Dahl draws on his own childhood experiences to create this sweet world. He was even a taster for a chocolate company!

Don't underestimate the power of chance! "Narnia" author C.S. Lewis saw an image of a faun carrying parcels and an umbrella in the snow when he was 16. This image haunted him for years before becoming the starting point for "The Chronicles of Narnia."

Children's imaginations are also a source of inspiration. Maurice Sendak, the author of "Where the Wild Things Are," based his book on his own childhood fears, turning his nightmares into a fantastical and educational adventure.

The everyday can also be magical. Beverly Cleary, tired of not finding books that speak of the life of ordinary children, creates Ramona Quimby, a character with whom every child can identify.

Myths and legends are not forgotten. Madeline Miller, in "Circe," takes the character of the witch from Homer's Odyssey and gives her a voice of her own, exploring her life before and after Odysseus's arrival.

And music in all this? Gayle Forman, the author of "If I Stay," is inspired by the emotional power of classical music to tell a poignant story of love and loss.

Sometimes, reality surpasses fiction. Angie Thomas draws from social reality and movements like Black Lives Matter to write "The Hate U Give," a book that opens eyes to inequalities and prejudice.

And for those who think fairy tales are outdated, Marissa Meyer proves otherwise. In "The Lunar Chronicles," she reinvents classics like Cinderella and Little Red Riding Hood in a futuristic world, proving that old tales can still be new and fascinating.

Social Networks

On March 21, 2006, Jack Dorsey, co-founder of Twitter, sent the first tweet in history: "just setting up my twttr". A simple declaration that heralded a revolution in online communication. Facebook, in its origins, was just an exclusive network for Harvard students, far from the global empire it has become. And Instagram, this showcase of perfect photos? It was once "Burbn", a check-in app akin to Foursquare.

Ah, Foursquare! Who remembers the frenzy to become "mayor" of a given place? Such an emblematic feature that it left a lasting impression, even though it has since been retired. LinkedIn, the serious professional network, succeeded where many failed: being profitable from its early years, thanks to its paid services.

TikTok, the global phenomenon, was once known as "Douyin" in China. Speaking of phenomena, MySpace was once the most visited website in the United States, even surpassing Google in 2006. A fact that may seem incredible today. Just like the story of Friendster, which turned down a $30 million purchase offer from Google in 2003. A decision that surely haunts the owners today.

WhatsApp, this omnipresent messaging app, had only 55 employees when Facebook bought it for the modest sum of $19 billion. Reddit, the "front page of the Internet", had to create an illusion of an active community in its early days, with its founders posting content under different pseudonyms.

And Vine? Despite its short lifespan, this platform launched the careers of many influencers who continue to thrive on other networks. Twitch, now synonymous with video game streaming, began as a humble live everyday life streaming platform called "Justin.tv".

Iconic Music Festivals

In 1969, Woodstock became the symbol of the '60s counterculture, drawing nearly 400,000 people to a muddy field in New York. Who could have predicted that what was to be a "small" gathering would become the epicenter for a generation seeking freedom and change?

Then there's Coachella, the Californian festival that has become an annual pilgrimage for lovers of music, fashion, and celebrity culture. And what about Tomorrowland in Belgium, where tickets sell out in minutes, as if it were a rite of passage for fans of electronic music.

Glastonbury, the venerable UK festival, combines the magic of music with that of the mystical ancient site of Glastonbury Tor. Burning Man, on the other hand, transcends the very notion of a festival. It's not just an event, but a sociocultural experience that sees the creation of a temporary city in the Nevada desert each year.

The Montreux Jazz Festival in Switzerland is like a living museum of music, having hosted legends like Nina Simone and Miles Davis. And in France, Rock en Seine had the dubious honor of being the stage for Oasis's last performance in 2009, marking the end of an era for the British band.

Lollapalooza began as a farewell tour for Jane's Addiction but is now a global festival. Fuji Rock in Japan, despite its name, moved from the majestic mountain to settle in the Naeba ski resort. And what about SXSW, the annual celebration of music, film, and technology in Austin, Texas?

Iconic Movies and TV Shows

Let's take "The Hunger Games" for example. Jennifer Lawrence, who portrayed the brave Katniss Everdeen, committed so deeply that she underwent intensive archery training. At the other end of the emotional spectrum is "Twilight," where Kristen Stewart nearly lost her iconic role as Bella Swan to Emily Browning.

Daniel Radcliffe, our beloved Harry Potter, was so invested in his role that he managed to break about 80 wands during filming. Who knew magic wands could also double as drumsticks?

The actors' commitment doesn't end there. Shailene Woodley, the star of "Divergent," not only cut her long hair for the role, but she also donated it to a charity. Talk about getting into character!

Some of these films and series go beyond entertainment, prompting public discussions on serious issues. For example, "13 Reasons Why" sparked numerous debates on its portrayal of sensitive topics such as suicide and bullying. Similarly, "Euphoria" has been both praised and criticized for its raw depiction of teenage life.

But these adaptations aren't just fictitious narratives; they often have real-world impacts. The film "Bird Box" spawned a viral challenge where people attempted to perform daily tasks blindfolded, highlighting the media's power to influence real-life behavior.

Each film or series is like a window into the complexities of adolescence, whether it's through exploring sexual identity in "Love, Simon" or portraying rare diseases like cystic fibrosis in "Five Feet Apart."

In addition to serving as a mirror to the complexities of youth, these cinematic adaptations and series also serve as a launchpad for young talents. Dylan O'Brien, the lead actor of "The Maze Runner," sustained a serious injury during filming that delayed production, but his career has only skyrocketed since.

Some films even introduce metanarrative elements that add an extra layer of depth to the story. In "To All the Boys I've Loved Before," the letter Lara Jean writes to Peter was actually an actress Lana Condor's farewell letter to her boyfriend, thus blending reality and fiction.

There are also moments when these works transcend the medium to become cultural phenomena. Take "Stranger Things," for instance. The setting of Hawkins is a time capsule of the '80s, paying homage to an era while capturing the imagination of a new generation.

Not to mention the impact of these works on popular culture. "The Kissing Booth" was not only a hit on Netflix, but it also made waves in real life when the main actors, Joey King and Jacob Elordi, started dating after filming.

Then there are films like "Lady Bird," which, while rooted in the teenage experience, speak to a much broader audience. Directed by Greta Gerwig, this film is a semi-autobiographical love letter to Sacramento, her hometown, and explores the delicate nuances of mother-daughter relationships.

Ah, the behind-the-scenes of Hollywood, a world as fascinating as the stories it produces! Emma Watson, who portrayed Hermione Granger in the "Harry Potter" series, was so committed to her role that she even wrote a multi-page essay on her character. Talk about total dedication!

You'd be surprised to know that "The Chronicles of Narnia" was as much a technical challenge as it was an artistic one. To bring the lion Aslan to life, creators used a mix of motion capture and special effects, raising the bar for future fantasy films.

Then there's "Percy Jackson." Logan Lerman, who portrayed the demigod hero, had to learn swordsmanship to make his character as authentic as possible. Yes, an actor's job isn't just about delivering lines!

The power of cinema is sometimes so strong that it changes lives. Take the film "Wonder," for example. It inspired the "Choose Kind" movement, encouraging kindness and acceptance in schools, thus transforming a simple story into a social movement.

And what about "Jumanji"? This film, based on a children's book, was so popular that it inspired several board game adaptations and even a sequel decades later, showing that some stories really do have incredible longevity.

Actors can also be fans! Millie Bobby Brown, who plays Eleven in "Stranger Things," is such a big fan of the "Harry Potter" saga that she asks for autographs from the actors when she meets them. This shows how interconnected these universes are in the entertainment world.

The social impact should not be overlooked. The film "Black Panther" was lauded for its positive representation of African culture and its role in the #BlackLivesMatter movement, proving that cinema can be a powerful force for change.

Some actors go beyond their on-screen role to get involved in real life. Amandla Stenberg, who played Rue in "The Hunger Games," has become an activist for civil rights, using her platform to raise awareness for various social causes.

Cryptography and Secret Codes

The Enigma machine used by the Germans during World War II had 159 quintillion possible settings.

Julius Caesar used a simple code to send secret messages, shifting each letter of the alphabet three places.

The RSA encryption technique was published by three researchers in 1978, but it was already secretly discovered by British intelligence years earlier.

The Book of Kells, a medieval work of art, contains cryptic text that no one has managed to decipher to this day.

The Phaistos Disc, an ancient clay tablet, uses mysterious symbols that have never been decoded.

During the Cold War, spies used "microdots," messages so small they could be hidden under the stamp of a letter.

Room 40 was a British decoding unit during World War I that managed to decipher many German codes.

The "Navajo code" was a code used by the Americans during World War II, based on the Navajo language, which was incomprehensible to the Japanese.

The Egyptians used hieroglyphs to write coded messages over 4,000 years ago.

The "Zodiac Letter" sent by a serial killer to newspapers in the 1960s contained a cryptic message that no one has been able to fully decipher.

In ancient Greece, messages were written on sheepskin that was wrapped around a stick. The message could only be read if one had a stick of the same diameter.

The Rosetta Stone helped researchers understand Egyptian hieroglyphs because it contained the same message in three different scripts.

Kryptos is a sculpture in the gardens of the CIA in Langley, Virginia, with four coded messages, three of which have been deciphered.

During World War II, carrier pigeons were used to transport encrypted messages across enemy lines.

The Spartans used a wooden rod called a "scytale" to code messages by wrapping a strip of leather around it and writing on it.

The "ROT13" method is a very simple code often used in online forums to hide spoilers. It shifts each letter by 13 places in the alphabet.

Modern hackers sometimes use a method called "quantum cryptography" which uses the properties of subatomic particles to secure messages.

The "Bacon's Cipher" is a 16th-century text that uses a code based on bold letters to hide a secret message, and some believe it could reveal that Francis Bacon is the true author of Shakespeare's works.

The Human Body

Heartbeats create enough energy to power a light bulb for an entire day. Imagine if your heart were a small power plant; it could light up a small lamp!

Your nose and ears never stop growing. While the rest of your body may stop growing at some point, these two parts continue their little adventure throughout life.

Saliva helps to pre-digest food before it reaches the stomach. Without it, eating would be a completely different experience. It also serves to clean and protect your teeth.

The stomach lining is so powerful that it can digest itself! Fortunately, new cells are constantly forming, renewing the stomach lining about every three days.

Your brain is more active at night than during the day. Even if you think your brain is resting while you sleep, it's actually very busy sorting through all the information from the day.

The longest bone in your body is the femur, which is as strong as concrete. It supports 30 times the weight of the human body, making it a solid pillar for walking, running, and jumping.

Humans and giraffes have the same number of cervical vertebrae. Despite their long necks, giraffes only have seven cervical vertebrae, just like humans.

The liver has over 500 functions and is the heaviest organ inside the human body. It's kind of like the body's chemical factory, helping to digest food, store energy, and remove toxins.

The human eye can distinguish about 10 million colors. It's almost like having a giant paint palette right in your eyes.

Each tongue has a unique print, just like fingerprints. If you've ever thought your fingerprints made you unique, wait until you see your tongue!

Hair can support about 100 grams each. Multiplied by the average number of hairs on a human head, this means your hair could support the weight of two elephants.

The sound made by cracking joints is actually caused by gas bubbles bursting in the joints. It's not dangerous at all, contrary to what some might think.

The human body contains enough iron to make a small nail. This metal is essential for helping to transport oxygen in the blood.

The skin is the largest organ of the human body. It serves as a protective barrier against germs and external elements, regulates temperature, and allows sensations of touch.

The bones of the skull are not completely fused at birth. That's why babies have "fontanelles," those soft areas on their head that allow some flexibility during childbirth.

The feet contain about a quarter of all the bones in the human body. If you've ever thought your feet were working hard, it's because they really are with all those bones.

Your brain does not feel pain. Even though it's the pain processing center in the body, the brain itself does not have pain receptors.

Humans lose an average of 40 to 100 hairs per day. Don't worry, they often grow back quite quickly, and with about 100,000 hairs on a human head, it's barely noticeable.

You breathe an average of 20,000 times a day. That's a lot of work for your lungs, which filter the air, humidify it, and send it into your body to keep you alive.

Humans have the ability to see objects in three dimensions because they have two spaced eyes. Each eye sees a slightly different image, and the brain merges them to create a 3D perception.

The History of Cinema and Special Effects

Georges Méliès, a magician turned filmmaker, is often regarded as the pioneer of special effects in cinema. His famous film "A Trip to the Moon" from 1902 utilized techniques such as stop-motion and painted backdrops.

The first color film was a short movie from 1908 called "A Visit to the Seaside". Before this, films were often hand-colored, frame by frame.

The term "blockbuster" originally comes from massive bombs used during World War II. It was first used in the 1940s in the film industry to describe a popular and successful movie.

The first female director in the history of cinema was Alice Guy-Blaché, who began making films in 1896. She even had her own film studio.

The lightsaber sound in "Star Wars" was created by combining the sound of a 70-year-old film projector and the noise of a tensioned cable being struck by a hammer.

The dinosaurs in "Jurassic Park" were not all digital special effects. Some were actually large puppets operated by people inside.

James Cameron's film "Avatar" used a new motion capture technology, allowing actors to see in real-time how their movements would translate into digital characters.

One of the oldest cinematic tricks is the "dissolve" transition, where one image slowly transforms into another. This trick was first used in 1903.

The film "The Matrix" is famous for popularizing the "bullet time" effect, where time appears to slow down. This effect was created using a series of cameras arranged in a circle around the action.

The first film to use synchronized sound was "The Jazz Singer" in 1927. Before this, films were silent and often accompanied by live music.

The character of Gollum in "The Lord of the Rings" was one of the first to be entirely created by motion capture, with actor Andy Serkis providing both the voice and movements for the character.

The first movie to use digital special effects (CGI) was "Westworld" in 1973. However, the first film to use CGI extensively was "Tron" in 1982.

The famous shower scene in Alfred Hitchcock's "Psycho" used chocolate syrup as fake blood because it looked better in black and white.

The phrase "It's a wrap" used at the end of filming comes from the days when films were shot on film reels. Once the filming was finished, the film was literally wrapped up and sent off for editing.

Frank Capra's film "It's a Wonderful Life" was one of the first to use artificial snow. Before that, filmmakers often used cornflour or cotton, but it was flammable.

The film "Inception" used a mix of digital special effects and physical sets to create its dream worlds. For example, the rotating hallway scene was achieved by building an actual rotating hallway.

In the early days of cinema, films were often projected onto white screens or even sheets. The projectors were so loud that they were usually placed in a separate room.

The movie "E.T. the Extra-Terrestrial" was so secretive during its production that the script was often written on colored paper to prevent unauthorized photocopies.

For the film "Toy Story", the creators had to invent a new form of CGI to create more realistic textures for the toys. It was the first time CGI was used for an entire movie.

The film "Snow White and the Seven Dwarfs" was the first full-length animated feature. Many thought it would be a failure, but it turned out to be a great success and paved the way for the animation film industry.

Iconic Women in History

Joan of Arc, at just 17 years old, led the French army to several significant victories during the Hundred Years' War against England. She was captured and burned at the stake, but she became a national heroine and a saint.

Marie Curie was a physicist and chemist who discovered the elements radium and polonium. She was the first woman to win a Nobel Prize and the only woman to have won Nobel Prizes in two different fields: Physics and Chemistry.

Rosa Parks, an African American woman in the United States, refused to give up her seat to a white passenger on a bus in 1955. Her act of civil disobedience was a pivotal moment in the Civil Rights Movement in the United States.

Harriet Tubman was a slave who escaped in 1849 and became a "conductor" on the Underground Railroad, helping other slaves escape to freedom. She also served as a spy for the Union Army during the American Civil War.

Frida Kahlo was a Mexican artist known for her self-portraits and unique style. Despite serious health issues and a devastating bus accident, she continued to paint until her death.

Helen Keller was born deaf and blind, but with the help of her tutor Anne Sullivan, she learned to communicate and became an inspiring author, activist, and lecturer.

Malala Yousafzai, a young Pakistani girl, was attacked by the Taliban for advocating for girls' rights to education. She survived and became the youngest Nobel Peace Prize laureate.

Cleopatra was one of the last pharaohs of ancient Egypt. She was also a skilled political strategist and diplomat who had liaisons with Roman leaders like Julius Caesar and Mark Antony.

Simone de Beauvoir was a French philosopher who wrote "The Second Sex," a foundational text in the development of feminism. She explored the ways in which women have been historically regarded as "the other" in a male-dominated society.

Amelia Earhart was an American aviator who was the first woman to fly solo across the Atlantic. She mysteriously disappeared while attempting to fly around the world, but her legacy inspired many women to pursue careers in aviation and other male-dominated fields.

Mother Teresa devoted her life to helping the poor and sick in Calcutta, India. She founded the Missionaries of Charity and was awarded the Nobel Peace Prize for her dedication to serving others.

Anne Frank was a young Jewish girl who hid with her family during World War II. Her diary, discovered after she died in a concentration camp, has become a poignant symbol of the suffering endured under Nazi occupation.

Soraya Tarzi, the queen of Afghanistan in the 1920s, was a staunch advocate for women's rights. She opened schools for girls and encouraged women to participate in public life.

Margaret Thatcher was the first woman to become Prime Minister of the United Kingdom. Nicknamed the "Iron Lady," she was known for her liberal economic policies and strong personality.

Emmeline Pankhurst was a British activist who fought for women's suffrage. She was known for her radical protest tactics and was imprisoned multiple times for her activities.

Billie Holiday was an American jazz singer who used her voice to fight against racism. Her song "Strange Fruit" about lynchings in the American South became an anthem for civil rights.

Benazir Bhutto was the first woman to lead a Muslim-majority country, serving as Prime Minister of Pakistan. Despite political challenges and corruption scandals, she remains an important figure in the struggle for women's rights in the Muslim world.

Olympe de Gouges was a French political activist and writer who was one of the first to demand women's rights during the French Revolution. She was executed for her radical views.

Katherine Johnson was an African-American mathematician who worked for NASA. She played a key role in the success of several space missions, including John Glenn's first human spaceflight orbiting Earth.

Sports

Basketball was invented by Canadian physical education teacher James Naismith in 1891. He was looking for an indoor sport to keep his students active during the winter and came up with the idea of hanging a basket on a wall.

Baseball, one of the most traditional sports, has been played in various forms since the 18th century. But did you know that the core of the first modern baseball was made from the material of a horse's shoe?

Cricket is so popular in India that the streets can be deserted during major matches. Sachin Tendulkar, considered one of the greatest cricket players of all time, is nearly a deity in India.

Ice hockey is Canada's national sport, but did you know that the first documented game took place in Montreal in 1875, and they used a rubber ball instead of a puck?

Surfing may look cool today, but it has been practiced for centuries in Hawaii. The first surfers used large wooden boards and surfed on huge waves as a spiritual ritual.

Scuba diving has become a popular sport, but did you know that the first autonomous diving gear was invented by Jacques Cousteau? It allowed divers to stay underwater for longer periods.

Wrestling is one of the oldest sports and was even practiced in the ancient Olympic Games. The rules were much simpler back then: the first to touch the ground with any part of the body other than the feet lost.

The Paralympic Games were created for athletes with physical disabilities. The first one took place in 1960 in Rome, and today, they follow the Olympic Games every four years.

Badminton is often played as a casual game, but at the professional level, the shuttlecock can reach speeds of up to 320 km/h! It's the fastest racket sport in the world.

American football has surprising origins. It was developed from rugby and soccer, and the first game was played between two American colleges in 1869. The game was so different that it would barely be recognizable today!

Skateboarding began as a pastime for surfers who wanted to "surf the streets" when the waves were too small. Today, it has even become an Olympic sport.

Judo is more than just a sport; it's also a philosophy. Created in Japan, it means "the gentle way" and teaches principles such as respect and discipline.

Formula 1 is not only a speed sport but also a sport of technology. The cars can cost millions of dollars and are designed with extreme precision to optimize every aspect, from fuel to aerodynamics.

Table tennis, often called ping-pong, has been an Olympic sport since 1988. Despite its small size, the ball can travel at speeds of up to 110 km/h in professional matches.

Parkour is a sport where the goal is to move from point A to point B as quickly as possible, using only the body to jump, climb, and roll. It was popularized in France and has since spread worldwide.

Music and Instruments

The piano has a fascinating history. Did you know that its ancestors are the harpsichord and the clavichord? The modern piano was invented by Bartolomeo Cristofori in Italy at the beginning of the 18th century, and it revolutionized classical music.

You surely know the violin, but did you know that its ancestor is the rebec, a medieval instrument? The violin appeared in Italy in the 16th century and was perfected by makers like Antonio Stradivari.

The harmonica is often associated with blues and folk music, but it has European origins. Invented in Germany in the 19th century, it was originally designed to play European folk music before becoming popular in the United States.

The electric guitar was invented in the 1930s, but it became iconic in the 1950s with musicians like Chuck Berry and Elvis Presley. Guitars like the Gibson Les Paul or the Fender Stratocaster have become legends in their own right.

The saxophone was invented by a Belgian, Adolphe Sax, in 1840. He wanted to create an instrument that would combine the strength of brass instruments and the gentleness of woodwind instruments. Today, the saxophone is an essential element of jazz and pop music.

The flute is one of the oldest known musical instruments. Flutes made from animal bones dating back to prehistoric times have been found. They already had holes for playing different notes!

The drum set is actually a collection of various percussion instruments brought together. Pieces like the bass drum, snare, and cymbals all have diverse origins, from Africa to Asia, and were combined to form the modern drum set.

The theremin is an innovative electronic instrument designed to be played without physical contact. Developed by Leon Theremin in 1920, this instrument uses two antennas to detect the position of the musician's hands and produce sounds. The hand movements in the space around the antennas modulate the pitch and volume of the sound produced.

The didgeridoo is an instrument of the Aboriginal Australians that may be over a thousand years old. It is made from a branch of eucalyptus hollowed out by termites and produces a deep, hypnotic sound.

The bagpipe is often associated with Scotland, but it has much older origins. The bagpipe is thought to have been created around 3,000 years ago in the Middle East before spreading to Europe.

The sousaphone is a type of tuba designed to be easier to play while marching. It was invented by the famous marching band musician John Philip Sousa, from whom it gets its name.

The harp is often associated with classical music and angels, but it is also an important instrument in Celtic music. Celtic harps are smaller and often decorated with ornamental designs.

The synthesizer has revolutionized modern music. It can mimic almost any instrument and create new sounds. Bands like Kraftwerk used synthesizers to create entirely new music genres.

Maracas are percussion instruments originating from Latin America. They are often made from dried fruits filled with seeds or pebbles and are used in music styles like salsa and reggae.

The ocarina is a small wind instrument shaped like a bird or a fish. It has ancient origins, from Chinese civilizations to Native American tribes. The sound of the ocarina is soft and melodic.

The accordion is a keyed and bellows instrument invented in Europe in the 19th century. It is used in a variety of musical styles, from French musette to Louisiana's Cajun music.

The zither is an ancient stringed instrument that was popular in ancient Greece. It is often depicted in Greek art and mythology and was associated with the god Apollo.

The djembe drum originates from West Africa and is made from a single hollowed-out tree trunk. It produces a wide range of sounds, from deep booms to sharp cracks, and is often used in drum circles.

The mandolin has Italian origins and became popular in the United States through bluegrass music. It has a shape similar to that of the violin but is played like a guitar.

The banjo has roots in Africa and was brought to America by slaves. It became a key element of American folk music and is known for its unique sound and complex playing technique.

Science

Water can exist in three different states: solid, liquid, and gas. But did you know that there is a fourth state of water called "supercritical water"? At extreme temperatures and pressures, water becomes a supercritical fluid with properties of both liquids and gases.

Shooting stars are not really stars. In reality, they are meteors burning up as they enter the Earth's atmosphere. If they survive the journey and land on Earth, they are called meteorites.

Sunlight takes about eight minutes and twenty seconds to reach Earth. This means that if the Sun suddenly went out, we wouldn't know it for eight minutes!

Ants are incredibly strong for their size. They can carry up to 50 times their own weight! Imagine carrying a car on your back, that's about the equivalent for an ant.

Volcano lava is not the only thing that can be dangerous. Volcanic gases like sulfur dioxide can be just as deadly. They can mix with water and create acid rain.

The human brain is made up of about 86 billion neurons. These neurons communicate with each other through small electrical signals. This is how we think, move, and feel emotions.

Lightning is so hot that it can instantly boil water! It can reach temperatures up to 30,000 degrees Celsius, which is five times hotter than the surface of the sun.

Carnivorous plants like the Venus flytrap don't just eat insects for fun. They do it because they often live in nutrient-poor soils and need other sources of nourishment.

There is a fascinating phenomenon called "murmuration" where thousands of birds, often starlings, fly together creating incredible shapes in the sky. This allows them to protect themselves from predators.

Earthworms don't have lungs. So how do they breathe? They use their skin! Oxygen passes through their moist skin and directly into their circulatory system.

Human DNA and banana DNA are surprisingly similar. In fact, about 60% of our DNA is identical to that of a banana! So next time you eat a banana, think of it as a distant cousin.

Magnets have a north pole and a south pole. If you cut a magnet in half, you won't get an isolated north pole and an isolated south pole. Each half will become a new magnet with its own north and south poles.

The venom of the black widow spider is actually more potent than that of a rattlesnake, but the black widow injects a much smaller amount, which generally makes it less dangerous to humans.

There are more bacteria in your mouth than there are human beings on Earth! But don't worry, most of them are harmless or even beneficial to your health.

Tornadoes can be incredibly powerful. The strongest can reach wind speeds of over 480 km/h and lift objects as heavy as cars!

Chameleons don't change color to blend into their environment. They do it primarily to communicate with other chameleons and to regulate their temperature.

Bees have five eyes! They have two large compound eyes on the sides of the head and three small eyes on the top. These small eyes help them to detect light and darkness.

The acid in your stomach is so powerful that it can dissolve a metal razor blade. Fortunately, the cells of the lining of your stomach regenerate quickly, which prevents the acid from digesting you yourself.

Sound travels faster in water than in air. That's why submarines use sonar to communicate or detect other objects underwater.

Total solar eclipses are rarer than you might think. On average, they only happen every 18 months somewhere on Earth. But for a given location, hundreds of years can pass between two total eclipses.

Theater and Performance

Chinese shadow theater is one of the oldest types of theater in the world. Using paper or leather silhouettes in front of a light source, artists tell stories that can be both simple and very complex.

Commedia dell'arte is an Italian type of theater where actors wear masks to represent stereotypical characters. These characters, like Harlequin and Pantaloon, have become archetypes in theater and literature.

Shakespeare's plays were often performed in broad daylight, not in the evening. The famous Globe Theatre in London had no roof, which meant that the shows were at the mercy of the weather!

Theater sets were not always as sophisticated as they are today. In the 17th century, a panel indicating "Forest" or "Castle" was often the only indication of where the scene was taking place.

The famous "iron curtain" in theaters is not just decorative. It is designed to be fire-resistant, in order to protect the audience in case of a fire on stage.

Mime Marcel Marceau saved children during World War II by using his mime skills to help them escape Nazi occupation. He guided them silently through forests and mountains to avoid detection.

Japanese kabuki theater uses a large number of special effects, called "keren". These effects can include quick costume changes or even stage elements that rotate and transform.

The term "vaudeville" does not refer to a style of performance, but to a type of entertainment. Vaudeville was a series of varied acts, such as comedy, dance, and magic tricks, often presented in a single show.

Street theater is a form of live art that takes place outside of traditional theater spaces. It can include anything from mime to juggling and is often used to address social or political issues.

Broadway in New York and the West End in London are considered the two biggest theater centers in the Western world. Yet, these two theater districts contain only a small fraction of the theaters in their respective cities.

Ancient Greek actors wore masks with cone-shaped mouths to help project their voice, like a megaphone, so everyone in the audience could hear them.

The "fourth wall" is an idea in theater that represents the invisible separation between the actors on stage and the audience. When an actor speaks directly to the audience, it is said that they "break the fourth wall".

Japan's Noh theater is one of the oldest styles of theater still practiced today. The actors wear elaborate masks and costumes, and the plays can often last all day.

The expression "Being in the spotlight" comes from the theater. Spotlights are used to highlight a specific actor or action on stage, thus drawing the entire audience's attention.

The Tony Award is one of the highest distinctions in the theater world. It was named in honor of Antoinette Perry, an actress, director, and co-founder of the American Theatre Wing.

Traveling theater troupes were common in the past. These troupes traveled from town to town to present shows, often under a tent or in ballrooms.

"Theater in the round" is a configuration where the stage is surrounded by seats on three or four sides, allowing the audience to have a more intimate view of the performance.

In France, the Comédie-Française, founded in 1680, is the oldest active theater company today. It has a monopoly on the performance of Molière's plays.

The term "dramaturgy" does not only concern the writing of plays, but also the study of the structure and form of drama. A "dramaturg" is often consulted during the production of a new play.

In theater, superstitions are taken very seriously. For example, it is considered bad luck to say the word "Macbeth" in a theater, except during rehearsals or performances of the play itself. It is often called "the Scottish play" to avoid the curse.

Anthropology

In some cultures, such as the Maoris in New Zealand, tattoos are not just aesthetic, but tell the story of the person and their family. The patterns are carefully chosen and each detail has a meaning.

The Aka pygmies of Central Africa are often cited as a fascinating example of active fatherhood. In this community, fathers spend more time caring for their children than in any other known society.

The Venice Carnival in Italy is famous for its elaborate masks. But did you know that each type of mask has a specific meaning? Some masks are intended to represent historical or mythological characters.

Rites of passage are ceremonies that mark important stages in life, such as adolescence or marriage. Among the Maasai in Africa, young boys must prove their bravery by hunting a lion.

The potlatch is a tradition of the indigenous peoples of the west coast of Canada and the United States. During these large feasts, hosts give gifts to guests, not to be generous, but to display their wealth and social status.

The Vikings were not just warriors, but also traders and explorers. They even reached North America well before Christopher Columbus, as evidenced by the archaeological remains found in Newfoundland.

In India, the tradition of yoga is more than 5,000 years old. It is not just a form of exercise, but a spiritual practice that aims to harmonize the body and mind.

Geishas in Japan are not "ladies of the night" as often thought, but are highly skilled artists in areas such as music, dance, and conversation.

Among the Amish in the United States, young people have a period called "rumspringa" in which they can explore the outside world before deciding to permanently join the Amish community.

In Inuit culture, the concept of "kunlangeta" refers to a person who lies, cheats, or steals. To help this person reintegrate into the community, they may be invited to a hunting party that also serves as therapy.

The San people of southern Africa use clicks in their language. These are sounds produced by sticking and unsticking the tongue from the palate, somewhat like the noise made to encourage a horse to move forward.

The Ainu are the indigenous inhabitants of some islands north of Japan. Unlike the Japanese, they have a different physical appearance and a unique culture that includes facial tattoos for women.

In Ethiopia, the Hamar tribe has a unique ceremony for young men coming of age. They must run across the backs of lined-up cows without falling, while the women of the tribe encourage them by singing.

In ancient Rome, the "vomitorium" was not a place to vomit after an excessive meal, as is often thought. It was actually an entrance or exit in an amphitheater, designed to allow spectators to quickly leave the venue.

In some Amazon tribes, when a person dies, their ashes or bones are sometimes mixed into food that the family then eats. It is a way for them to keep the deceased alive in their memory.

In Papua New Guinea, there is a tribe called the Asaro or "mud men". To scare their enemies, they cover themselves in mud and wear terrifying masks made of clay.

The Sámi people in Scandinavia have been herding reindeer for centuries. Reindeer are so important to them that they have hundreds of different words to describe the various parts of the animal's body.

In ancient Greece, the Spartans had a strict military education from a young age. Children were tested at birth and only the strongest were kept to become warriors.

In China, the tradition of foot binding in women was considered a sign of beauty and high social status. Fortunately, this painful and dangerous practice is now banned.

Laws

In Vermont, USA, it is illegal to hang laundry on a public sidewalk. This law may seem odd, but it exists for safety and hygiene reasons.

In France, it is illegal to name a pig Napoleon. This law dates back to the time of Napoleon Bonaparte and aimed to prevent ridicule of the great statesman.

In Saudi Arabia, there are no rivers, but it is still illegal to fish in a spring or well without permission. This law is in place to protect the country's limited water resources.

In the UK, it is illegal to die in the Houses of Parliament. Technically, this is because anyone who dies there must be given a state funeral, which could be complicated.

In the state of Oregon, USA, hunters may not use lassos to catch fish. Yes, you heard that correctly, lassos!

In Singapore, the sale of chewing gum is banned to keep the streets clean. This law has been relaxed for sugar-free gum, but violations can still lead to heavy fines.

In Canada, if you have to pay a fine, it is illegal to do so using only one-cent coins. This law aims to prevent cumbersome payments.

In Switzerland, it is illegal to flush the toilet in an apartment after 10 p.m. This law is there to maintain peace and quiet.

In Turin, Italy, it is mandatory for dogs to be walked at least three times a day. This law aims to ensure the welfare of pets.

In Thailand, it is illegal to step on money. The king's face appears on banknotes and coins, and stepping on it would be considered disrespectful to the monarchy.

In the state of Alabama, USA, it is illegal to play dominoes on Sunday. This law is a relic of the "blue laws" that regulated Sunday activities.

In Australia, it is illegal to name an animal that you intend to eat. This law seeks to prevent emotional attachment to the animal.

In Hawaii, it is illegal to stick a coin in someone's ear. The reason for this unusual law remains a mystery.

In Denmark, it is not allowed to start a car without first checking if someone is underneath. This law is there for safety reasons, although it seems a bit excessive.

In Greece, electronic games were banned from 2002 to 2011 in an effort to combat illegal gambling.

In Arizona, USA, donkeys cannot sleep in bathtubs. This law dates back to an incident where a donkey was swept away by floodwaters while sleeping in a bathtub.

In Rome, it is illegal to drive a cart without brakes. This law dates back to Roman times and is still in force.

In Brazil, it is illegal to make noise with a samurai sword in a cinema. This law aims to reduce distractions during movies.

In Tuszyn, a small town in Poland, it is illegal to bring Winnie the Pooh into a children's playground. Authorities believe the fictional bear is poorly dressed and has questionable morals.

In China, it is illegal for Buddhist monks to reincarnate without government permission. This law is in place to control the monastic population.

Businesses

The term "freelance" originates from the medieval period where knights who were not pledged to any lord were referred to as "free lances". Today, it refers to someone who works independently, without a long-term contract with an employer.

In 1987, the first ever registered domain name was Symbolics.com. It belonged to a computer manufacturing company but now serves as a financial information website.

The word "boss" comes from the Old French "baston", meaning "stick". Originally, a "stick" was a measure of work done, so the "boss" was the one who kept track of the work.

Toyota's brand logo is actually a clever design that contains all the letters of the word "Toyota". Created in 1990, it is intended to symbolize the company's global vision.

The first credit card was created because its inventor, Frank McNamara, forgot his wallet during a business dinner. Embarrassed, he conceived a way to pay without cash and launched the Diners Club Card in 1950.

Bitcoin was created by an individual or group of people using the pseudonym Satoshi Nakamoto. Despite numerous attempts to uncover their identity, it remains a mystery.

The first product sold online was a Sting CD, purchased in 1994. E-commerce was still in its infancy, and the CD took a week to be delivered!

The concept of "Happy Hour" originated on American Navy ships in the 1920s. It was a time for entertainment for sailors, and now it's a widely used term for discounts at bars and restaurants.

Jeff Bezos founded Amazon in his garage in 1994. Originally, the company sold only books, but it quickly expanded to become the online retail giant we know today.

Toblerone bars were designed to resemble the Swiss Alps. Their creator, Theodor Tobler, was a Swiss chocolatier with a passion for the mountains.

The first television advertisement was broadcast in 1941, before a baseball game. It lasted only 20 seconds and cost the advertiser nine dollars.

The word "business" comes from the Old French "entreprendre", meaning "to undertake something". The term has evolved over time to denote an organization that aims to make money.

Starbucks got its name from the character Starbuck in the novel "Moby Dick". The founders were looking for a name that evoked the romance of the high seas and the rich seafaring heritage of Seattle.

The famous Nike "Swoosh" logo was designed by a graphic design student for just 35 dollars. Today, it is one of the most recognized logos in the world.

The term "bribe" comes from the Old French "pour boire", which was a sum of money given to buy a drink. Today, it's a term for an illegal payment to gain an advantage.

The first vending machine was invented by an Egyptian priest in the first century. It dispensed holy water in exchange for a coin.

The word "salary" comes from the Latin "salarium", which was the money given to Roman soldiers for the purchase of salt. Salt was a valuable commodity at the time.

In business, a "black sheep" is an investment that yields poor or negative returns. The phrase comes from the notion that black sheep were less valuable than their white counterparts because they provided wool of an undesirable color.

"Cyber Monday" was created by online retailers in 2005 to encourage people to shop online. It follows "Black Friday" and has become one of the most profitable days for online commerce.

Politics

During its construction, the White House in the United States was not white but gray. It was painted white after being partially burned during the War of 1812 against the United Kingdom.

The word "candidate" comes from the Latin "candidatus," which means "clothed in white." In ancient Rome, those running for public office wore white togas to stand out.

The clock tower of the British Parliament is often called Big Ben, but in reality, Big Ben is the name of the bell inside the tower. The tower itself is called Elizabeth Tower.

The term "veto" comes from Latin and means "I oppose." In ancient Rome, a "veto" was a way for an official to block a decision made by another.

In some countries, like Australia, voting is mandatory. If you do not vote, you may be subject to a fine or even community service.

The nuclear button is not actually a button. In the United States, the president must use a set of codes and protocols to launch a nuclear attack. It's much more complicated than just pressing a button.

The word "politics" comes from the Greek "polis," which means "city" or "state." Politics is, therefore, literally the affairs of the city or state.

The youngest elected president in the United States was John F. Kennedy, who was 43 years old when he took office. The oldest is Joe Biden, who was 78 at his inauguration.

The concept of "democracy" was born in Athens, Greece, over 2500 years ago. The word means "power of the people," and it was a way for citizens to participate directly in the decisions of their city.

Iceland is the country with the oldest continuously functioning Parliament in the world. It was established in the year 930 and is called the Althing.

The first woman elected as the head of a country was Sirimavo Bandaranaike of Sri Lanka in 1960. She was followed by many other female leaders around the world.

Napoleon Bonaparte was not really short. The rumor of his short stature is due to a conversion error between the French and British measuring systems. He was about 1.69 meters tall, which was average for his time.

The "Space Race" during the Cold War was not just a technological competition but also a demonstration of political and ideological power between the United States and the Soviet Union.

Before becoming president of the United States, Ronald Reagan was a movie actor. He even starred in a film with a monkey named Bonzo!

The word "senator" comes from the Latin "senex," which means "old" or "elder." The Senate was seen as an assembly of wise elders in ancient Rome.

The notion of "right" and "left" in politics comes from the French Revolution. Supporters of the king sat to the right of the assembly president, and the revolutionaries sat to the left.

Nelson Mandela spent 27 years in prison before becoming the first black president of South Africa. He became a global symbol of resistance to oppression.

The flag of the United Nations was adopted in 1947 and features a map of the world surrounded by olive branches, symbolizing peace and international cooperation.

The "smiley" ☺ was first used in politics by a candidate for mayor of New York in 1953. It was printed on badges to make the candidate more approachable.

The word "lobbying" comes from the lobby or hall of hotels and government buildings where people waited to speak to politicians. Today, it's a common practice to influence political decisions.

Flag

The flag of Nepal is the only national flag that is not quadrilateral. It consists of two stacked triangles, symbolizing the Himalayan mountains and the country's two main religions, Hinduism and Buddhism.

Did you know that the pirate flag, the famous "Jolly Roger" with a skull and crossbones, had a meaning? It was designed to frighten and intimidate the crews of merchant ships, encouraging them to surrender without a fight.

The Brazilian flag is quite unique. The 27 small stars in the blue circle represent the 26 Brazilian states and the Federal District. The stars are arranged as they appeared in the sky over Rio de Janeiro on November 15, 1889, the day the Republic of Brazil was proclaimed.

The Canadian flag, with its maple leaf, is relatively new. Before 1965, Canada used the "Red Ensign," which included the Union Jack and the Coat of Arms of Canada. The new flag was adopted to represent Canada independent of its colonial ties.

The Union Jack, the flag of the United Kingdom, is a combination of the flags of England, Scotland, and Northern Ireland. Each of these countries has its own cross, and they are all included in the Union Jack.

The white stripe in the middle of the French flag symbolizes royalty, while the blue and red represent the city of Paris. During the French Revolution, these colors were adopted as a symbol of liberty, equality, and fraternity.

The Greek flag has nine blue and white stripes symbolizing the nine syllables of the national motto: "Freedom or death." The blue represents the sea and sky, while the white represents the purity of the struggle for independence.

The Indian flag has its saffron stripe for courage, white for peace and truth, and green for fertility and prosperity. At the center is a 24-spoke wheel, called the "Ashoka Chakra," representing the eternal cycle of life.

The Australian flag has the Union Jack in the upper left corner to symbolize its connection with the United Kingdom. The five stars on the right represent the Southern Cross, a constellation visible in the Southern Hemisphere.

The Jamaican flag is the only national flag that contains neither blue, red, nor white. It has green for the wealth of the land, black for the people, and gold for the sunlight.

The Swiss flag is one of only two square flags in the world, the other being that of Vatican City. The white cross on a red background is a symbol of protection and defense.

The red stripe of the Austrian flag is often said to symbolize the blood shed in the battles for the country. However, there is no definitive proof of this origin.

The United States flag has 13 stripes for the original 13 colonies and 50 stars for the current 50 states. It is said to have been designed by Betsy Ross, a Philadelphia seamstress, according to legend, but this story is widely considered a myth.

The Danish flag, called the "Dannebrog," is the oldest national flag still in use. According to legend, it fell from the sky during a battle in 1219 to encourage Danish troops.

The Finnish flag, with its blue cross on a white background, symbolizes the country's lakes and snow. The blue also represents loyalty to the country.

The Japanese flag, known as the "Nisshōki," represents the sun. The red circle symbolizes an uninterrupted sun, representing equality and simplicity.

The South Korean flag has a yin-yang in the center, surrounded by four trigrams. These elements come from Taoism and Confucianism and represent balance and harmony.

Medicine

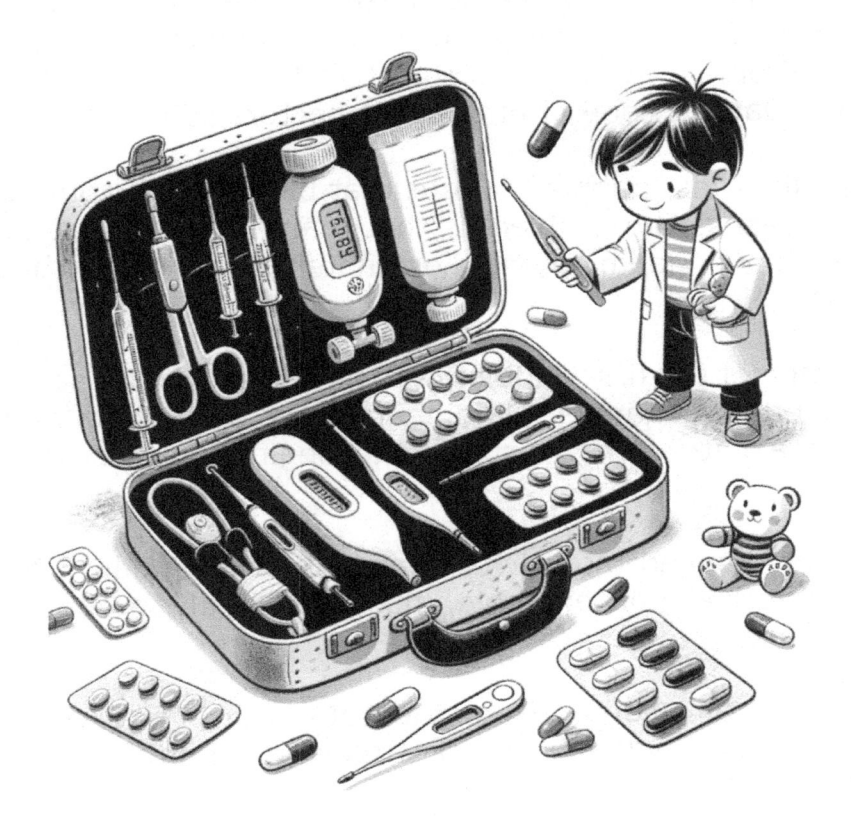

The first human heart transplant was performed in 1967 by South African surgeon Christiaan Barnard. The operation was such an event that people gathered around radios and televisions to follow the news.

The process of bone renewal in the human body is a continuous phenomenon where bone tissue is constantly broken down and reformed. About every ten years, the entirety of the bone is renewed through this regenerative activity. This means that the skeleton you have today is not exactly the same as the one you had a decade ago.

In ancient Egypt, doctors used flies to help heal wounds. They believed that flies could clean the wound and accelerate the healing process. Today, we know that this is a very bad idea because of the germs that flies can carry.

Hippocrates, often considered the "father of medicine," was the first to suggest that diseases were not caused by supernatural forces, but by environmental and biological factors. He also wrote the Hippocratic Oath, a code of ethics that doctors still follow today.

In the Middle Ages, people thought that bloodletting could cure all sorts of diseases. The problem is that many patients lost so much blood that they ended up dying. Fortunately, this practice has fallen into disuse.

Penicillin, one of the first antibiotics, was discovered by accident. In 1928, scientist Alexander Fleming noticed that mold had killed bacteria in a Petri dish. This was the beginning of a new era in medicine.

Vaccines have saved more lives than any other medical tool. The smallpox vaccine, for example, has completely eradicated this deadly disease.

The term "doctor" comes from the Latin word "medicus," which means "one who heals." It was first used in a Roman poem in the first century AD.

General anesthesia was used for the first time in 1846. Before that, surgeons had to perform operations while the patients were still conscious, which was incredibly painful.

The stethoscope was invented in 1816 by a French doctor named René Laennec. Before that, doctors had to put their ear directly on the patient's chest to listen to the heartbeat.

In some cultures, traditional healers use methods like singing, dancing, and even trance to help heal the sick. These methods are often combined with medicinal plants.

Aspirin, one of the most used drugs in the world, is made from willow bark. The ancient Egyptians and Greeks already used willow bark to reduce fever and relieve pain.

X-rays were discovered in 1895 by Wilhelm Conrad Röntgen. He received the first Nobel Prize in Physics in 1901 for this revolutionary discovery that changed the face of diagnostic medicine.

The first MRI scanner was used in 1977. Before that, doctors often had to resort to invasive methods like surgery to see inside the human body.

The first ultrasound was performed in 1956. This technique uses sound waves to create an image of the inside of the body, which is particularly useful during pregnancy.

The survival rate for many serious diseases, like certain types of cancer, has significantly increased thanks to advances in medicine. For example, the 5-year survival rate for breast cancer has gone from 63% in the 1960s to nearly 90% today.

Robotic surgery has become increasingly common. These robots are controlled by surgeons and allow incredible precision, thus reducing the risks and recovery time for patients.

In the 1800s, dentists often used gold wires to make dental fillings. Today, a variety of materials are used, including composites that resemble natural teeth.

The first home pregnancy test was marketed in the 1970s. Before that, women had to go to the doctor for a pregnancy test, which was often expensive and less convenient.

The World Health Organization (WHO) was established in 1948 and is part of the United Nations. Its goal is to build a world where everyone has the highest possible level of health.

Aliens and UFOs

Mysterious lights in the sky to tales of close encounters, the topic of aliens and UFOs has always been fascinating. Did you know that the term UFO stands for Unidentified Flying Object? It's not necessarily an alien spacecraft!

Project Blue Book was a serious study conducted by the U.S. Air Force to investigate UFOs. Over 12,000 sightings were collected, but the project found no definitive evidence of extraterrestrial visitors.

In 1947, a rancher in New Mexico discovered strange debris on his land. The military first said it was a crashed UFO but later retracted the statement. This event is known as the "Roswell Incident" and still sparks debate.

There is a "World UFO Day," celebrated on July 2nd, to raise awareness about UFOs and extraterrestrial life.

Some astronauts, like Edgar Mitchell, the sixth man to walk on the Moon, have stated they believe in the existence of aliens and think that the government is withholding information.

SETI is a scientific project that uses large radio telescopes to listen for alien signals. Just imagine if we one day received a message from space!

The "Wow! Signal" is a radio signal picked up in 1977 that was considered the best candidate for an alien signal. It has never been explained or redetected.

The movie "E.T. the Extra-Terrestrial" by Steven Spielberg was so popular that it even influenced the way we picture aliens: small, with big heads and large eyes.

There's a theory called the "Fermi Paradox" that wonders why, with so many planets in the universe, we still haven't found signs of extraterrestrial life.

The oldest UFO report dates back to 1440 BC in Egypt. The scribes of Pharaoh Thutmose III described "circles of fire" in the sky.

Betty and Barney Hill were a couple who claimed to have been abducted by aliens in 1961. Their story is one of the most famous in terms of alien abductions.

The "Black Knight Satellite" is a conspiracy theory about a 13,000-year-old alien satellite orbiting Earth. Of course, there's no solid evidence to support this.

There's a United Nations treaty that states if a human being makes contact with an alien, they must inform the UN. Seriously, it's called the Outer Space Treaty!

UFOs have even been spotted by presidents! Jimmy Carter and Ronald Reagan both claimed to have seen unidentified objects in the sky.

In 2020, the U.S. Department of Defense declassified three videos showing encounters between Navy fighter jets and what they call "unidentified aerial phenomena."

The word "extraterrestrial" is often shortened to "ET," which stands for "Extra-Terrestrial" in English. This word became very popular, especially after the movie of the same name.

The book "Chariots of the Gods" by Erich von Däniken suggests that ancient technologies and religions were brought to Earth by aliens. Many scientists disagree, but the book has captured the imagination of many.

The "Popocatepetl," an active volcano in Mexico, is often associated with UFO sightings. Videos show strange objects entering or exiting the crater.

The Arecibo message is a radio transmission sent into space in 1974 aiming to contact extraterrestrials. The message contains basic information about humans and Earth. Imagine if we received a reply!

The Power of Colors

Red is often associated with energy, passion, and action. In some cultures, it's even the color of happiness and luck. In China, red is a lucky color often seen at weddings and festivals.

Did you know that blue is the favorite color of most people in the world? It's a color that evokes calm and serenity, like a blue sky or a peaceful sea.

Yellow is the most visible color to the human eye, which is why it's used for traffic signs and safety vests. This color often evokes optimism and positivity.

In color psychology, green is associated with nature, growth, and regeneration. In hospitals, rooms are often painted green because it is considered soothing.

Purple was once so expensive to produce as a pigment that only kings and queens could afford to wear clothing of this color. Today, it is often associated with creativity and imagination.

Black and white are not really considered colors in the light spectrum, but they have a huge impact in design. Black is seen as elegant and formal, while white evokes purity and simplicity.

In some cultures, pink is associated with femininity, but this has not always been the case. In the early 20th century, pink was even considered a masculine color!

Colors can also affect our appetite. Studies have shown that red and yellow stimulate the appetite, which is why many restaurants use these colors in their logo or decoration.

The color orange is a mix of red and yellow, and it combines the energies of these two colors. It is often associated with enthusiasm and adventure.

Colors can also have an effect on our mood. Studies have shown that people work better and feel more comfortable in spaces with soothing colors like blue or green.

There is a therapy based on colors called chromotherapy. This practice uses colors to adjust imbalances in the body and mind.

The flags of countries often have colors that have specific meanings. For example, the blue on the French flag represents freedom, the white equality, and the red fraternity.

The term "having a blue fear" comes from the ancient belief that ghosts and spirits were visible in blue in the moonlight.

Have you ever heard of the expression "blue Monday"? It's a way of describing the feeling of sadness that some people feel at the beginning of the work week.

Some colors are associated with specific causes. For example, pink is often used to raise awareness of breast cancer and red for the fight against AIDS.

In the animal world, colors play an important role in survival. The chameleon changes color to camouflage itself, while the peacock uses its colorful feathers to attract a mate.

The color of our skin is determined by a pigment called melanin. The more melanin, the darker the skin. It's a natural adaptation to different climatic conditions and levels of sunlight.

Gold is a color associated with wealth and luxury. In ancient Egypt, gold was considered the flesh of the gods and was used to make death masks for pharaohs.

In sports, teams often wear bright colors to stand out. Team colors can even affect performance. One study showed that teams wearing red win more often!

The word "color" comes from the Latin word "color", which means appearance or complexion. It makes sense, as colors play a big role in how we see and understand the world around us.

Incredible Machines

Did you know that the world's largest bulldozer weighs more than 68 tons? It's so powerful that it can move 76 tons of material in a single pass!

The Large Hadron Collider in Switzerland is the world's largest particle accelerator. It has a circumference of 27 kilometers and allows scientists to study the smallest particles that make up our universe.

You've surely seen a helicopter, but have you ever heard of the Mi-26 quadrotor helicopter? It's so large that it can carry another helicopter inside its cargo bay!

Hyperloop is a new form of transportation that could allow us to travel at speeds of up to 1200 km/h. Imagine, you could go from Paris to Marseille in less than 30 minutes!

Giant cranes are used to build skyscrapers and other huge structures. The largest crawler crane can lift the equivalent of 20 school buses at the same time!

The space shuttle is an impressive machine that has allowed humans to travel into space. It can take off like a rocket and land like an airplane.

The combine harvester is an agricultural machine that can harvest, thresh, and clean grain in one operation. It's like a giant Swiss Army knife for farmers!

The Bagger 288 excavator in Germany is the world's largest mobile land machine. It's so large that it has to be assembled on-site and can extract enough coal in one day to fill nearly 2400 coal trucks.

The tunnel boring machine is used to dig large tunnels. The world's largest tunnel boring machine, nicknamed "Bertha," has a diameter of nearly 18 meters.

Drones are small flying machines that can be remotely controlled. They are used for everything from package delivery to aerial photography.

The steam engine revolutionized industry and transportation. Did you know that the first steam locomotive was built in 1804?

The hoverboard is a kind of futuristic skateboard that floats above the ground. Although it's not as advanced as the ones seen in movies, it is being developed.

Submarines can explore ocean depths where humans cannot go. The submarine that has reached the most extreme depth is capable of diving to depths exceeding 10,000 meters below the ocean's surface.

The Da Vinci robot allows surgeons to perform complex operations with incredible precision. The robot is remotely controlled by the surgeon using a command console.

The wind turbine is an amazing machine that turns wind into energy. Some of the largest wind turbines can generate enough energy to power 600 American homes.

The tram is a form of public transport that uses rails like a train but operates in the city like a bus. In Bordeaux, the tram uses a special technology that allows it to run without visible overhead lines.

The jet pack is a device you wear on your back that allows you to fly. It is still in the testing phase, but imagine being able to fly over traffic jams to get to school!

Roller coasters are machines designed to give us thrills and excitement. The fastest in the world reaches a speed of 240 km/h, faster than many sports cars!

The Castle

Have you ever seen a castle in a movie or a book and thought, "Wow, I'd love to live there!"? But did you know that the first strongholds were actually wooden and earth structures, built to defend against enemies?

The world's largest castle is Malbork Castle in Poland. It covers an area of 21 hectares, which is like 30 football fields put side by side!

Strongholds often had moats filled with water around them to prevent invaders from entering. Some even had fish in their moats, like a decoration and a source of food.

Castles were very lively places, with markets, churches, and even knights' tournaments. It wasn't just the home of the lord and his family, but also a small community.

Have you ever heard of the Tower of London? It's a stronghold that has served as a prison and even a zoo! Exotic animals such as elephants and lions were kept there.

Strongholds often have watchtowers where sentinels can keep an eye on the surroundings. From above, you can see very far, which is useful for spotting approaching enemies.

The walls of castles are often very thick to withstand attacks. Some walls are even more than a meter thick!

The drawbridge is one of the coolest parts of a castle. It's a bridge that can be raised or lowered. When it's raised, no one can enter or exit the castle.

Castles had secret rooms called "oubliettes" where they locked up prisoners. It's a bit like the secret hiding spots you might have in your room, but a lot less nice.

Battlements are those small openings at the top of castle walls. They allowed archers to shoot arrows while being protected.

Castles often have chapels because religion was very important at the time. Some chapels were even built to resemble small castles!

Castles were often surrounded by gardens and farmland. They had their own farms, vineyards, and sometimes even mills.

Castles often have coats of arms that represent the family that lives there. Each symbol has a special meaning, a bit like the emojis you use when you send messages.

In some castles, there were rooms reserved for baths. Yes, even knights and kings needed to take baths!

The throne room is where the king or queen received guests and made important decisions. It was a bit like the living room of the house, but much more grandiose.

The kitchens in castles were huge! They had to prepare food for hundreds of people every day. Imagine having to prepare a meal for your whole class every day!

Castles often had ramparts, which are large walls that surround the castle. You could walk on them and they also served as defense.

Some castles had very ingenious heating systems. They used giant fireplaces and ducts to distribute heat to different rooms.

Banquet halls were where everyone gathered to eat and party. Imagine a birthday party, but almost every day!

Some castles even had their own brewery to make beer. But don't worry, the kids drank a much weaker version than the adults.

Castles were often built on hills or near water to have a strategic advantage. From the top of a hill, you can see enemies coming from afar!

Castles often had multiple gates and complicated paths to access them. It was done on purpose to confuse invaders and make them easier to stop. It's a bit like a giant maze!

Unexplained Natural Phenomena

There's a lake in India where human skeletons are found every year when the ice melts. It's believed these people died from a hailstorm hundreds of years ago, but no one is certain.

Have you ever seen a rainbow? Well, in some places, you can see a full circle! It's very rare and it's due to light refraction, but it's so beautiful that some people think it's magical.

And what about the northern lights? Those lights in the sky that dance like ghosts. They're caused by solar particles, but some cultures believe they're the work of spirits or gods.

In the desert, there are rocks that move all by themselves! They're called "sailing stones," and even though it's thought that wind and ice have something to do with it, no one has ever seen them move.

In Antarctica, there's a lake under the ice that's so salty it never freezes. It's called "Blood Falls" because the water is red due to the minerals.

In some countries, there are fires that have been burning for thousands of years. They're called "eternal flames," and even though it's thought they're fueled by natural gases, it's still a mystery.

There are underwater rivers in the oceans. Imagine that, a river within another river! They even have trees and leaves on their "banks."

There are giant holes in some lakes that swallow everything nearby. They're called "sinkholes" and they're super dangerous.

In some forests, there are trees that bend for no apparent reason. It's not known if it's natural or the work of humans, but it's really strange.

In Venezuela, there's a place where there are storms almost every night. It's called the "Catatumbo lightning," and it's an incredible sight to see.

In the Namib Desert, there are circles in the sand that no one can explain. They're called "fairy circles," and some think they're made by extraterrestrials.

There are pink lakes in Australia. Their color is due to algae and shrimp, but it's so surprising that it looks like another world.

In Norway, there are giant whirlpools in the sea. They're called "maelstroms," and they can be very dangerous for ships.

In Siberia, there are giant craters that appear overnight. It's thought they're caused by gas explosions, but it's not certain.

In some marshes, there are lights that float in the air. They're called "will-o'-the-wisps," and even though it's thought they're caused by decomposing gas, they're still a bit spooky.

In Mexico, there's a cave full of giant crystals. Some are even bigger than a bus! It's not known how they were able to grow so large.

In the Pacific, there are islands that disappear and reappear. It's thought to be due to volcanic activity, but it's still a mystery.

And finally, there are places where it snows even in summer. They're called "perpetual snows," and even though it's because of the altitude, it's always surprising to see snow in the middle of July!

Lost Civilizations

Did you know that there was a civilization called Sumer in Mesopotamia? They invented writing, but one day, they just vanished. We don't really know why, it's like they just disappeared into thin air.

Ah, and the Mayans! They were super advanced in mathematics and astronomy. They even created a very precise calendar. But at some point, they just stopped building pyramids and carving stelae, and we don't know why.

There's also the Indus Valley civilization. They had well-planned cities with sewage systems and everything, but they disappeared without a trace. Some think it was due to climate change, others say invasions.

The Minoans lived on the island of Crete and were known for their luxurious palaces. But they were wiped out by a volcanic eruption or maybe a tsunami, we're not sure.

Have you ever heard of Atlantis? It's an island that supposedly existed a long time ago but was swallowed by the ocean. Some people think it really existed, but no one has ever found proof.

There was a civilization in Africa called the Kingdom of Kush. They were so powerful that they even conquered Egypt at one point. But eventually, they disappeared and we don't quite know why.

The Anasazi were people who lived in the southwestern United States. They built homes in cliffs, but at some point, they just stopped and vanished.

The Phoenicians were great sailors and traders, but their civilization disappeared and we don't know where they went or what happened to them.

The Kingdom of Aksum in Ethiopia was very wealthy due to trade, but it was destroyed, perhaps because of climate change or overexploitation of the land.

The Olmecs were one of the earliest civilizations in America and are known for their huge stone heads. But they disappeared before the Mayans even became powerful.

The civilization of Carthage in North Africa was so powerful it nearly beat Rome. But eventually, Rome destroyed Carthage and everything that was left of it.

The Etruscans in Italy were very advanced, but they were conquered by the Romans and their culture was almost entirely lost.

There was a people called the Toltecs in Mexico who were very influential, but they disappeared and we don't know why.

In China, there was a civilization called Sanxingdui that left behind strange bronze masks, but we know nothing else about them.

The Scythians were nomadic horsemen who lived in what is now Russia. They left behind tombs filled with treasures, but their culture disappeared.

In Peru, the Nazca civilization is known for its giant lines in the desert that can only be seen from the sky. But we don't know why they made them, or what happened to them.

The Celts lived all over Europe, but when the Romans and other peoples invaded, they disappeared or were assimilated.

There was a civilization called Mississippian in North America that built huge mounds, but they vanished before Europeans arrived.

The people of the Tiwanaku civilization near Lake Titicaca in Bolivia disappeared, leaving behind mysterious statues and temples.

Ah, and let's not forget the Maoris of New Zealand. They built huge statues called Moai, but we don't know how they did it or why their civilization declined.

Mathematics in Nature

You know, mathematics is not just in books or classrooms; it's everywhere in nature. Take the Fibonacci sequence, for example. Have you ever seen a sunflower? If you count the spirals in one direction and then the other, you'll get two consecutive numbers from the Fibonacci sequence. Incredible, isn't it?

And seashells! Have you noticed that many have a spiral shape? This spiral is actually a logarithmic spiral, and it follows a very precise mathematical formula. Even the waves of the ocean follow mathematical patterns when they break on the beach.

Snowflakes are another fascinating example. Each snowflake has a symmetrical hexagonal structure, which is a mathematical characteristic. And yet, each snowflake is unique.

Do you know about fractals? These are shapes that repeat infinitely, and we can find them in things like ferns or trees. Even mountains and clouds can be described using fractals.

Let's talk about bees. Their hives are built in hexagons, and there's a mathematical reason for that. The hexagon is the shape that uses the least material to create a storage space, so it's the most efficient.

And the stars in the sky? The orbits of planets around the sun follow very precise mathematical laws, discovered by astronomers like Kepler.

Spirals are very common in nature, such as in hurricanes or galaxies. These spirals often follow the rule of the golden number, which is another mathematical concept.

Even in our bodies, mathematics plays a role. For example, the rhythm of our heart follows complex mathematical patterns.

Spider webs, you might find them scary, but they are actually masterpieces of geometry. Spiders use the least amount of silk possible to create a web that covers the largest area.

The patterns on the fur of animals, like the stripes of a zebra or the spots of a leopard, can also be explained by mathematical equations.

Have you ever seen schools of fish or flocks of birds? They move in patterns that can be described by mathematical algorithms.

The branches of trees and the way they divide also follow mathematical patterns. This allows the tree to receive as much sunlight as possible.

Crystals are natural forms that have a very orderly structure. This structure can be described using geometry and algebra.

Even sound has a mathematical dimension. Sound waves can be described by mathematical equations, and that's why we can create music.

The patterns found in fruits and vegetables also follow mathematical rules. Like sunflower seeds, apple seeds are arranged in circles that follow the Fibonacci sequence.

The way light moves and refracts follows mathematical laws. That's why we can see rainbows.

DNA in our cells has a double helix structure, which is actually a very complex mathematical shape.

Geological formations, like stalactites and stalagmites in caves, also follow mathematical patterns in their formation.

Even anthills are built following mathematical algorithms. Ants follow very precise rules to maximize the efficiency of their colony.

Chess and Checkmate

Ah, chess is not just a simple board game. It's an entire universe of strategies, tactics, and even mathematics. Did you know that there are more possible moves in a game of chess than there are atoms in the known universe? This is known as "combinatorial complexity," and it's dizzying!

Chess has a fascinating history. It originated in India over a thousand years ago under the name chaturanga. The game traveled the world, from Persia to Europe, changing and evolving. Even Napoleon Bonaparte was a fan of this mind game!

Let's talk about openings, those crucial first moves that can decide the entire match. There are hundreds, with names like the Sicilian Defense or the Spanish Opening. These names often come from the players or countries that popularized them.

You might wonder why the squares on the chessboard are black and white? It's not just to look pretty. The contrasting colors help players better visualize movements and strategies.

Chess grandmasters are like rock stars in the chess world. They have an incredible memory and can recall entire games, move by move, even years later.

Some pieces are more powerful than others, but did you know that the queen wasn't always so strong? Before, she could only move one square at a time. It wasn't until the 15th century that she became the most powerful piece on the board.

There are even robots that play chess! In 1997, a computer named Deep Blue beat world champion Garry Kasparov. Since then, computers have become increasingly strong, but they also help humans improve.

Chess is also an excellent brain exercise. Playing regularly can improve your memory, concentration, and even your math skills.

Chess is not just a man's game. Great players like Judit Polgár have beaten several male world champions. She was even one of the highest-ranked players in the world, men and women combined.

Did you know there is a version of chess where the pieces are placed randomly at the start of the game? It's called Chess960, and it was invented by world champion Bobby Fischer to make the game even more interesting.

The term "checkmate" comes from the Arabic "shah mat," which means "the king is helpless." And that's the whole point of the game, to put the opposing king in a position where he can neither flee nor be saved.

The scholar's mate is one of the oldest tricks in chess to trap a beginner. In just four moves, you can checkmate the opposing king if the other player is not careful.

There's a rule called "en passant" that many people don't know about. It allows a pawn to capture another pawn that has just jumped two squares in front of it, as if it had only jumped one.

Stalemate is a rare situation where a player has no legal move to play, but their king is not in check. The game then ends in a draw, with no winner or loser.

In some tournaments, players have a time limit to make all their moves. This is called "speed chess," and it makes the game even more stressful and exciting.

The king can also jump over a rook to get to safety, but only if neither piece has yet been moved. It's called "castling," and it's a good way to protect your king.

The cheapest piece is the pawn, but if you manage to get one of your pawns to the last row of your opponent's side, it can be promoted to any piece. Most of the time, players choose another queen.

Movies and series, like "The Queen's Gambit," have made chess even more popular. This series even caused an increase in chess set sales worldwide.

Chess is so popular that there are even games played by correspondence. Players send their moves by postal mail, and a game can last months or even years!

There are chess tournaments for all ages and levels. Some young prodigies, like Magnus Carlsen, started playing in tournaments when they were just a few years old.

Playing chess can even make you travel. International competitions take place all over the world, from New York to Moscow to Dubai. Who knows, maybe you'll be the next grandmaster to tour the world!

The Art of Camouflage

The art of camouflage isn't just for spies or soldiers! In nature, many animals use camouflage to hide from predators or to hunt. The chameleon, for instance, can change the color of its skin to blend into its surroundings. It's like wearing an invisible suit!

The term "camouflage" comes from the French word "camoufler," which means "to disguise." During World War I, armies began to use camouflage techniques to hide their soldiers, vehicles, and even ships. Artists were even recruited to create deceptive patterns and colors.

Mimicry is when an animal or plant looks like another object or living being. Some butterflies, for example, have wings that resemble dead leaves. So, they can land on a branch and disappear almost completely!

You might have seen cars or planes with strange patterns of geometric shapes and different colors. These patterns are designed to confuse the eye and make it difficult to gauge the object's distance.

In the world of film and video games, optical camouflage is often used to create special effects. For example, an actor can wear a green suit against a green background, which then allows them to be replaced with any other setting using digital techniques.

Thermal camouflage is when special materials are used to hide body heat. This can be very useful for escaping thermal cameras that detect heat instead of colors.

Marine animals also have their own camouflage techniques. Some flatfish can bury themselves in the sand, leaving only their eyes sticking out. Others, like squid, can even change texture to resemble aquatic plants!

Camouflage clothing has become fashionable, but it has a very serious origin. The patterns are designed to help soldiers blend into different environments, like the forest, desert, or snow.

Researchers are working on "chameleon" materials, which change color based on their environment. Imagine being able to wear a t-shirt that changes color on its own!

The cheetah, the fastest land animal, uses camouflage to approach its prey without being seen. Its spots resemble the shadows and lights of the African landscape, making it almost invisible when stalking.

Leaf-cutter ants have developed a very special camouflage technique. They carry pieces of leaves over their heads to hide from predators while they work.

In modern art, some artists use camouflage to reflect on the way we see the world. They can paint objects or people to blend into a setting, creating a fascinating illusion.

Camouflage isn't just for hiding; it can also be used to scare. Some animals, like pufferfish, can swell up and show patterns that resemble giant eyes to scare away predators.

Engineers study animal camouflage techniques to apply them to human technologies. For example, drones might one day use mimicry techniques to go unnoticed.

Children love to play hide-and-seek, and it's a form of camouflage! Finding the best place to hide and staying quiet is practicing the art of concealment.

Henna, a natural dye, is sometimes used to create camouflage patterns on the skin. It's an ancient tradition in some cultures to celebrate special events.

The military sometimes uses camouflage nets to hide vehicles or equipment. These nets are designed to resemble the local vegetation, making them nearly undetectable from a distance.

Crab spiders are pros at camouflage. They can adjust the color of their body to match the flower they're on. Thus, they can catch insects without being seen.

Orchid mantises are incredible insects that resemble flowers. They use their appearance to attract pollinating insects, which then become their meal!

The Months of the Year

Did you know that the names of the months of the year have fascinating origins that date back centuries? January, for instance, comes from the Roman god Janus, who has two faces. He looks both towards the past and the future, just like we do when a new year starts!

February gets its name from the Latin word "Februarius," which is related to "februa," an ancient Roman festival of purification. It's often the month when we start thinking about the big spring cleaning!

March is named after Mars, the Roman god of war. Maybe it's because this is the month when nature "fights" to come out of winter and welcome spring.

April might come from the Latin word "aperire," which means "to open." It's the month when flowers start to open and spring really arrives.

May is named after Maia, an earth goddess and a goddess of growth. It's the month when everything seems to grow and bloom.

June comes from "Juno," the queen of the gods in Roman mythology. She is the protector of marriage and the well-being of women, which might explain why many people choose to get married in June.

July was named in honor of Julius Caesar, the famous Roman general. Before, it was called "Quintilis," which means "fifth" in Latin, because it was the fifth month of the Roman calendar.

August owes its name to Augustus, the first Roman emperor. He chose this month because he won several of his great victories in August.

September, October, November, and December come from the Latin words for seven, eight, nine, and ten. It's a bit strange because they are actually the 9th, 10th, 11th, and 12th months of the year! This is because the original Roman calendar started in March.

In some cultures, months have completely different names that are linked to the seasons or agricultural activities. For example, in the traditional Japanese calendar, one of the months is called "Yuki-gedzuki," which means "month of melting snow."

In the past, some people used a lunar calendar based on the moon's phases. In this system, each month began with the new moon. This is still the case for the Islamic calendar.

You may have heard of a "blue moon," which is a month with two full moons. The term "once in a blue moon" comes from there and means that something is very rare.

In the Aztec calendar, there was an extra month every four years, much like our leap year. Except this month had only five days!

In Russia, during the 1917 revolution, the country switched from the Julian calendar to the Gregorian calendar. As a result, people woke up one morning to find that they had "jumped" from February 1st to February 14th!

Some months are associated with precious stones or flowers. For example, if you were born in May, your stone is the emerald and your flower is the lily of the valley.

In Ethiopia, the calendar has 13 months! Twelve months of 30 days and a thirteenth month of 5 or 6 days, depending on whether it's a leap year or not.

The "International Movement for a Rationalized Calendar" proposed a calendar with 13 months of 28 days each, plus an extra "zero day." But the idea never really took off.

In the Hebrew calendar, some months have a "twin"! For example, there are two months called Adar in a leap year. The second is added to keep the calendar aligned with the seasons.

The Balinese calendar, used in Bali, Indonesia, has only ten months! But watch out, each month has 35 days, so the year is actually longer.

Months and their names are a whole story that travels through time and cultures. So the next time you turn the page of your calendar, you'll know that each month has its own little secret to tell!

Precious Stones

Precious stones have always fascinated humans. They are more than just colorful pebbles; they have stories to tell and powers that some believe to be magical! Take the diamond, for example. Did you know that it's made entirely of carbon, the same element that's in the pencil you use to draw? The only difference is the way the carbon atoms are arranged.

The emerald is known for its beautiful green color. But did you know that this color comes from chromium and vanadium in the stone? Yes, these metals change everything!

Some gemstones, like opal, can display a whole range of colors. In fact, some opals can shine with all the colors of the rainbow when light hits them in a certain way.

Turquoise is a gemstone that has been used to create jewelry for thousands of years. The ancient Egyptians loved it so much that they even used it to decorate the funeral masks of mummies!

Moonstone is truly special. It has a kind of blue glow that moves when you turn it, a bit like the phases of the moon. That's why it's called moonstone.

If you like legends, you'll love the story of lapis lazuli. In ancient Mesopotamia, this stone was considered sacred and was believed to have the power to guide the soul into the afterlife.

Amethyst is a purple stone that was once as precious as ruby and emerald. Today, it's much more affordable, but just as beautiful. In antiquity, it was believed to protect against drunkenness!

The gemstone called alexandrite is truly amazing. It changes color depending on the light. In daylight, it's green, but under artificial lighting, it turns red!

Garnet is often red, but it can also be green, orange, yellow, or even purple. What's even cooler is that under certain conditions, it can even look like a little rainbow!

Quartz is a gem appreciated for its diversity of colors, capable of adopting almost every shade imaginable. One of the fascinating varieties is "cat's eye quartz," characterized by a central luminous band. This feature gives it the striking appearance of a feline's eye.

Some gemstones, like peridot, come from space! Yes, you heard right. They are brought to Earth by meteorites.

Labradorite has an incredible play of colors that looks like the northern lights captured in a stone. The colors change depending on the angle at which you look at it.

Spinel is often confused with ruby. In fact, some of the world's most famous gemstones, once thought to be rubies, turned out to be spinels!

Agate is a really cool gemstone because it has layers of different colors. It's like a rainbow-colored cake, but in stone!

Jade has been used to create tools and jewelry since prehistoric times. In Chinese culture, it is associated with purity and morality.

Topaz can be colorless, but it is often treated to take on all sorts of colors, from blue to pink to golden.

Coral isn't really a stone; it's actually the hardened skeleton of marine creatures! It is often used to make jewelry and can be red, pink, or white.

Tanzanite is a gemstone discovered in Tanzania in the 1960s. It is so rare that it's considered a thousand times rarer than diamond!

Zircon is one of the oldest substances on Earth. Zircons found in Australia are about 4.4 billion years old. That's almost as old as the Earth itself!

And there you have it, a little guided tour into the fascinating world of gemstones. They are much more than pretty decorations; they are the silent witnesses to the history of our planet and the cultures that have cherished them.

Street Art

Street art, or urban art, is not just an explosion of colors on walls. It's a form of expression that gives a voice to the voiceless. Artists like Banksy have even achieved superstar status by creating works that make people think.

In some cities, entire neighborhoods are transformed into open-air art galleries. In Berlin, the Berlin Wall has become a massive canvas where artists from around the world come to leave their mark.

Graffiti, one of the forms of street art, is actually very ancient. The ancient Romans engraved messages on the walls of their cities. So, this art form has survived through the ages!

Street art can also be ephemeral. Some artists use chalk or even natural materials like leaves and branches to create works that last only a few hours or days.

Stenciling is a very popular technique in street art. It allows artists to quickly and easily reproduce a design. Banksy, one of the most famous artists in the street art world, uses this technique a lot.

In some cases, street art can even be in 3D! Artists like Edgar Mueller create incredibly realistic drawings on the ground that give the illusion of being three-dimensional.

Street art is not just visual. Some artists use sound as a form of street art. They install hidden speakers to surprise and amuse passersby.

Some street artists work at night to avoid being caught by the police, as in many places, painting walls without permission is illegal. But for these artists, the risk is worth it!

Some street art projects are true collaborative works. The "Before I Die" project invites people to write their hopes and dreams on a large blackboard.

Street art can also be a way to raise awareness of social or political causes. In Palestine, artists use art to draw attention to the hardships of life under occupation.

In some cities, street art is so appreciated that it is protected and preserved. In Melbourne, Australia, there are even "laneways," or small alleys, where street art is encouraged and celebrated.

Street art can also be interactive. Some artists create works where people can add their own drawings or messages.

Yarn Bombing is a form of street art where public objects like trees or lampposts are covered in knitting or crochet. It's a soft and cozy way to transform the urban landscape!

Street art can also be digital. With the rise of augmented reality, artworks can be superimposed on the real world through a smartphone screen.

Street art can sometimes become a treasure hunt. Artists hide little treasures or messages in their works for the public to discover.

In street art, even the basic materials can be surprising. Some artists create works of art from chewed gum or waste found on the street.

Some street artists are so skilled at trompe-l'oeil that their creations seem to come out of the wall or dive into the ground. This often leads to incredible photos!

Street art can also be humorous. Some artists like to play with existing elements, such as road signs, to create funny or ironic situations.

There are even street art festivals where artists can showcase their works and the public can learn to create their own. It's a beautiful way to celebrate this art that is accessible to everyone.

Street art is one of the freest and most democratic forms of art. No need for a ticket or gallery, just a walk down the street to be touched, surprised, or inspired. So, the next time you take a stroll, keep your eyes wide open! Who knows what masterpiece you might discover?

Recycling

Recycling isn't just about tossing bottles and cans into a special bin. It's a real adventure for objects! Imagine a plastic bottle becoming a t-shirt or a park bench.

Did you know that paper can be recycled up to seven times? After that, the fibers become too short to make new paper. But even then, they can be used to create other things like egg cartons.

In some countries, there are machines where you can deposit plastic bottles and get money in return. It's a nice way to encourage people to recycle while earning a little pocket money!

Glass is amazing! It can be recycled indefinitely without losing quality. So the juice bottle you drink today could have a second life as a window or even as jewelry!

Old car tires don't always end up in a landfill. They can be transformed into flooring for playgrounds, insulation materials, or even shoes!

The screens of our phones and computers contain precious metals like gold and silver. By recycling them, we can recover these materials and use them to manufacture new devices.

Did you know that food scraps can be turned into energy? In some factories, food waste is converted into biogas, which can be used to produce electricity.

Aluminum cans are super quick to recycle. In just 60 days, a can can be collected, melted down, and turned into a brand new can ready for use.

Clothes can be recycled too! Some are turned into rags for industry, while others are broken down to create new textile fibers.

Remember floppy disks? These old storage media are now obsolete, but the plastic and metal they contain can be separated and recycled to create new objects.

Artists use recycled materials to create incredible works of art. From sculptures to paintings, recycling can also be a source of artistic inspiration.

Coffee grounds are not just for throwing away. They can be used as fertilizer for plants, as a deodorant, and even to grow mushrooms!

Old newspapers and magazines can have a second life as packaging material or can be transformed into papier-mâché for artistic projects.

Some toys are made from recycled plastic. It's a way to give a second life to objects that could have ended up in the trash.

Plastic toothbrushes can be recycled into new products like benches, cutting boards, and even trash cans!

There are pens that are made from recycled plastic bottles. Each pen uses the equivalent of one bottle, which helps to reduce waste.

CDs and DVDs that are no longer used can be recycled into building materials or even jewelry. Who would have thought that these old discs could have such a glamorous new life?

Used cooking oil should not be poured down the sink as it can clog pipes. But it can be recycled into biodiesel, a more environmentally friendly type of fuel.

Companies use recycled fishing nets to create sportswear. It's a way to remove these nets from the ocean where they can harm marine life.

Printer ink cartridges can be recycled to make new ones. Some companies even offer discounts if you bring back your old cartridges.

Modes of Transportation

Trains can be faster than you might think! In France, the TGV (Train à Grande Vitesse) can reach speeds of up to 320 km/h (about 199 mph). That's like zooming at breakneck speed on rails!

Hot air balloons aren't just for cartoons or history books. They've been around since the 18th century and were among the first forms of air transportation. Imagine floating above fields and cities, carried by the wind!

Electric cars aren't a modern invention! The first electric car was created in the 1830s, well before gasoline-powered cars. And they're making a big comeback today to help protect our planet.

Bicycles have evolved a lot over the years. There are even bikes that can float on water! They have special floats and paddles instead of wheels, so you can pedal on rivers and lakes.

The world's largest airplane has a wingspan wider than a football field! The Antonov An-225 Mriya was built to transport really, really heavy loads, like space shuttles.

Scooters aren't just for kids. Nowadays, there are electric scooters that even adults use to quickly get around cities, especially during rush hour.

Cruise ships are like floating cities. Some are equipped with swimming pools, cinemas, restaurants, and even basketball courts and mini-golf courses!

Helicopters can take off and land without a runway. This makes them super useful for rescue missions in hard-to-reach places, like mountains or at sea.

Dog sleds are still used in some parts of the world, especially in very cold regions. These dogs are incredibly strong and can run for hours in the snow.

Airships, those big balloons filled with gas, were very popular at the beginning of the 20th century. They're coming back into fashion for certain uses, like surveillance or even tourism.

Skateboards aren't just for tricks. In some cities, people use them as a means of transportation to get to work or school.

Segways, those funny machines you stand on, are becoming increasingly popular for city tours. They're electric and can go quite fast!

Trams were very common in cities around the world before buses and cars arrived. Some cities have kept their old trams as a tourist attraction or have modernized them for more eco-friendly public transportation.

The world's smallest airplane is only 1.68 meters long and has a wingspan of 1.88 meters. Flying in such a tiny craft must be an incredible experience!

Pedal boats, those small boats operated by pedals, are a fun and ecological way to get around on water. Perfect for a peaceful ride on a lake!

Underwater scooters are like scooters for the water. They have small engines that help you swim faster and explore the ocean floor without getting too tired.

A funicular is a type of train that can climb very steep slopes thanks to a cable. They are often found in the mountains or in cities built on hills.

Horse-drawn carriages were once the main means of transportation in cities. Today, they are mostly used for tourist rides or special occasions.

Solar cars use the power of the sun to move. They have solar panels on the roof that capture sunlight and convert it into electricity to drive the car.

Pets

Dogs are known to be man's best friend, but did you know they have a sense of smell that is 40 times more powerful than that of humans? It's as if they had super-noses!

Cats can make incredible jumps. Some can jump up to five times their own height in a single leap. Imagine a cat jumping almost as high as a door!

Hamsters love to exercise, especially at night. That's why they love their wheel so much. Some can run up to 9 km (about 5.6 miles) in their wheel in a single night.

Goldfish have a much better memory than many people think. They can remember things for up to five months and can even be trained to perform tricks.

Parrots don't just repeat the words they hear. Some can understand the meaning of these words and even use simple phrases to communicate with humans.

Rabbits love to play games like hide and seek. They also have a unique way of showing they're happy by doing a jump in the air and twisting themselves, called a "binky."

Ferrets are small, very curious, and playful animals. They love to explore tunnels and hiding spots, and can even be trained to do small tricks.

Turtles can live a very long time, some up to 100 years or more. It's like having a pet that could be as old as your great-grandfather!

Guinea pigs love company and can even become sad if they are alone. They also like to "talk" by making small noises to communicate with each other or with their owner.

Iguanas are exotic animals that can change color according to their mood or environment. They are mostly active during the day and enjoy climbing and exploring.

Mice are very intelligent little rodents. They can solve mazes and even use simple tools to get food.

Snakes can sense their environment using their tongue. They flick it out to pick up particles in the air, then fold it back to analyze them with a special organ in their mouth.

Frogs have permeable skin, which means they can breathe and even drink through their skin. But this also makes them sensitive to water pollution.

Pet snails, like the African giant snail, can grow up to 20 cm (about 8 inches) long. And even though they're slow, they're also very curious and like to explore their environment.

Canaries are known for their melodious singing, especially the males. They sing to attract a partner and mark their territory, and each canary has its own "style" of singing.

Spiders are not insects, but arachnids. Some people keep them as pets and find them fascinating, especially with their ability to weave complex webs.

Rats are very social and intelligent animals. They enjoy playing and solving problems, and they can even understand complex concepts like sharing and empathy.

Lizards, like the gecko, can lose their tail to escape a predator and then grow a new one. It's not magic, but rather an incredible adaptation to wild life.

Hedgehogs are small mammals covered in spines. They roll into a ball to protect themselves, which makes them almost impossible to catch for predators.

Bees can be somewhat unusual pets, but some people enjoy raising them for their honey. And bees are super important for the pollination of plants.

Dear readers,

I recently fulfilled a dream by publishing my book. As an independent publisher, every step of this journey has been an exciting challenge, and knowing that I can count on your support is incredibly valuable to me.

If my book has touched, inspired, or brought you joy, I would be extremely grateful if you could share your experience. Your feedback is not only valuable to me as an author, but also helps other readers discover my work.

Here's how to leave a review:

1. Go to the item's detail page on Amazon by visiting
2. Select Write a Product Review in the Customer Reviews section.
3. Choose a rating for the book.
4. Once you have written your review, a green check mark will indicate that your opinion has been successfully submitted.
5. You can also add text, photos, or videos before selecting Submit.

Your review can make all the difference and will help me continue to write and share my stories. Thank you immensely for your time and support.
With all my gratitude

Made in the USA
Las Vegas, NV
14 December 2023